What Others Are Saying
About Reggie White . . .

—— *"The Best Player in the NFL"*

"It's almost impossible to be the best player without playing one of the most important positions, so that eliminates everyone who isn't a passer or a pass rusher and leaves Reggie White and Joe Montana as the finalists. And White, the Philadelphia Eagles' defensive end, gets the nod. They're both in their prime, but at 34, Montana is six years older and much less likely to stay there for five more years. To win one game, which player would you want on your team? Lawrence Taylor would be the answer to that one, as he demonstrated by carrying the overmatched Giants into overtime against the Rams in last year's playoffs. Taylor can still disrupt an entire offense, running and passing, all by himself, but he can't still do it 16 straight weeks. White plays at a consistent level that isn't far behind Taylor's best. He does everything a defensive lineman can be asked to do. He's an end in the base defense, but he moves inside a lot in the Eagles's 46 defense. He's a human detour sign to the running game, and he's the best pass-rushing lineman in the game. The only reason he doesn't have more sacks is that the Eagles don't find it necessary to move him along the line in search of good matchups. They've got the other pass-rushers, so they let White take the triple-team, turn loose Clyde Simmons and Jerome Brown, and wind up with three sackers in double figures. When his situation was more comparable to that of Tim Harris' three years ago, White responded with 21 sacks, only one short of the league record in his strike-limited 12 games. Like all the best players, White makes his good teammates look a lot better."

Sport Magazine, October, 1990

—— *"The Perfect Defensive Lineman"*

"If you had to make the perfect defensive lineman, you would take Reggie's ingredients and then you'd have him. He's probably the most gifted defensive athlete I've ever been around, and I've been around a lot of good ones."

Buddy Ryan

—— *"Reggie Never Disappoints as a Role Model"*

"A lot of people looking for role models in this world are often disappointed, but Reggie never disappoints as a role model. He's somebody you can hang your hat on."

John Spagnola, Offensive Lineman, Philadelphia Eagles

—— *"They Forget About His Strength"*

"People are so worried about his speed because he is so fast that they forget about his strength. They try to get out there and set up before he beats them with speed, so they are a little off-balance and he'll just throw them over. I've seen him put those 300-pounders on their rearend a bunch of times. I get a kick out of that."

Ron Heller, Offensive Lineman, Philadelphia Eagles

—— *"Reggie White Has No Equal"*

"Reggie White has no equal, he's the Rolls-Royce of defensive lineman. I came into this league in 1969, and I've only seen one defensive lineman I'd put in his category—Deacon Jones. Deacon Jones wasn't as good against the run, but he flashed in the pass rush like this guy. And Reggie can do it with both power and finesse."

Dick Vermeil, former Eagles Coach, ABC-TV analyst

—— *"He's Unbelievable"*

"Reggie White [is the best defensive lineman in the game today], of course. Who else? He's unbelievable, there's no question about it. Did I hesitate when I said his name? No, nobody would. He's unbelievable."

Jim Burt, Nose Tackle, San Francisco Forty-Niners

—— *"The Jerry Rice of NFL Defenders"*

"[Reggie White] is the Jerry Rice of NFL defenders, you can never stop him completely, just try to limit the damage he can cause."

Gridiron Magazine, October, 1989

Reggie White

MINISTER OF DEFENSE

WITH

TERRY HILL

Wolgemuth & Hyatt, Publishers, Inc.
Brentwood, Tennessee

The mission of Wolgemuth & Hyatt, Publishers, Inc. is to publish and distribute books that lead individuals toward:

- A personal faith in the one true God: Father, Son, and Holy Spirit;

- A lifestyle of practical discipleship; and

- A worldview that is consistent with the historic, Christian faith.

Moreover, the Company endeavors to accomplish this mission at a reasonable profit and in a manner which glorifies God and serves His Kingdom.

Wolgemuth & Hyatt, Publishers, Inc.
1749 Mallory Lane, Suite 110
Brentwood, Tennessee 37027

Library of Congress Cataloging-in-Publication Data

White, Reggie.
   Reggie White : minister of defense / Reggie White and Terry Hill.
   —1st ed.
       p. cm.
   ISBN 1-56121-087-0
   1. White, Reggie. 2. Football players—United States—Biography.
3. Philadelphia Eagles (Football Team) I. Hill, Terry II. Title.
GV939.W43A3 1991
796.332'092—dc20
[B]
                                                                91-25383
                                                                CIP

This book is dedicated to
Sara Copeland White, my wife,
the greatest gift that God has ever
blessed me with,

and

to Jeremy and Jecolia White,
my two beautiful children,
whom God uses to teach me
about a father's love.

I'll love you all forever.

CONTENTS

vii

Part Four: Final Score

ACKNOWLEDGMENTS

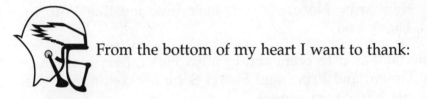 From the bottom of my heart I want to thank:

Thelma Collier, my wonderful mother;

Christie Collier and Julius Dodds, my sister and brother;

Leonard Collier, my stepfather; Charles White, my father;

Jannette and Jackie, for putting up with me for many years;

Vanessa, for being like a sister, cuz;

Ronnie Dodds, my uncle;

Mildred Dodds, my very special grandmother, the backbone of the whole family, whom I love very much;

Ida White, for supporting me and Sara through trials;

The White family for your love to me before and after;

Aunt Christy, for being the example I needed in order to ask Jesus into my life;

Reverend Ferguson, for planting a seed in my heart when I was nine years old;

Herman Prater, for always thinking of me;

Coach Robert Pulliam, for getting football skills out of me I didn't even know I had, and for believing in me when nobody else did;

Jackie Davidson, for helping me build my life;

Jesus Christ, for what You did for me on the Cross. I've treated others like dirt at times, but You still love me. For not allowing me to compromise with the world's standards. No one could ever love me like You do. Thank You!

Special thanks to Brent and Cynthia Fuller, Jerry and Janice Upton, and Bruce and Sheryl Sofia for continued discipleship of Sara and me.

For my always supporting family: Charles and Maria Copeland, Sara's parents and fantastic grandparents to Jeremy and Jecolia; Mark, Elizabeth, and Shari Copeland; Wayne, Maria, and Wesley Dozier; Chris, Patrice, and Paige Tillison; and Lamar, Dee, Stevie, and Jamal Galloway.

Many thanks to these special friends: Cedric, Lisa, Joshua and Jessica; Tom and Jenny; Mike and Yalonda; Buddy and Joan Ryan, Eric, Annie, Tiesha, Sequona, William, and Jessica; Chubby and Kathy; Gary and Correta; Don, Lisa, and Kristen; the Hood family; Rollins family; Davis family; Oliver family; Jackie and Betty Sue; Charlisa; Mr. and Mrs. Bishop; Veola and Fred; R. V. and Frances; John, Lisa, and Gina; Greg and Val; Calvin, Devorah, and Josh; Fernando, Jennifer, and Danniele; Jackie and Betty Sue; Valerie Hood; Lee Jenkins; Frosty and Miki; Art and Gail; Frank and Nadine; Ron and Sheila; Herman and Lawanda; Carey, Susan, Landon, and Shane; Mark and Mona; Alan and Jackie; Kyle and Mary Lynn; Merrill and Cindi; J. Paul, Kathy, and the A Team; Glen and Linda; Steve and Lisa; Henry and Rose; Mike and Andy; and Debbie Wehner.

Thanks for your hard work toward our ministry: Terry and Dianne Hill; Kyle Rote; Jimmy Sexton and Peggy; Pat Stewart; Frederick and Delores Brabson.

Also, many thanks to NFL Films; A.R.M.; Inner City Ministries; Ron Howard; and Rich Burg.

PART ✦ ONE

FOOTBALL

O•N•E

LESSONS OF THE CHATTANOOGA PROJECTS

Hawaii. Perfect temperature, low humidity, gorgeous flowers, and breathtaking scenery. What an incredible opportunity to play in my first Pro Bowl.

In 1987, my first pro season, I had reached a milestone of every professional football player's career—to be voted to participate in the Pro Bowl after my first complete season in the NFL. Man, was I excited!

Then came a bombshell. Joe Ward, a friend who directs the Lay Witnesses for Christ program which Willie Gault and I had helped in fund raising, gave me some terrible news. Two young people who were working on a roast in my honor were killed in a car accident.

I immediately turned to my wife Sara and told her that I was going to play as hard as I possibly could and win the Most Valuable Player trophy for this family.

By the time the game started, I was wound tighter than a drum, ready to unleash every ounce of energy in my body during this football game. On the first play I ran through the guy trying to block me and almost sacked the Bronco's John Elway in the end zone. And it would not be the last time John and I would be face-to-face that day.

By the fourth quarter, I had sacked John Elway twice and the Dolphins' Dan Marino once, tying the Pro Bowl record for most sacks in a game. My goal was clear: I was determined to break that record for sacks.

I lined down in front of all-pro offensive tackle Cody Riesen of the Cleveland Browns. Cody had effectively kept me away from his quarterback until Mr. Elway, in one of his patented moves, broke out of the pocket. When I saw him sprint out to the side, I immediately eluded my blocker and took off like a man possessed.

Although Elway's back was to me, he saw me, and so he sprinted to his right to evade me. But on this play, Reggie White would not be stopped. I ran him down, caught him from behind, and with a quick maneuver forced him to the turf.

As I hurried to the sideline after the play, a sense of peace came over me as I realized that I had accomplished my goal for playing in the Pro Bowl. A few moments later the announcer broadcast over the sound system my name as the Most Valuable Player of the 1987 Pro Bowl. As I accepted congratulations from my teammates, I also prayed that God would be with the family of those friends who died in the car mishap.

A Tough Start

How in the world could a little guy from the projects in Chattanooga, Tennessee, achieve such a goal, having his name recognized by every football fan in the country? Dreams combined with hard work really do come true.

Every child in the projects in Chattanooga or in any other inner city hopes to get out one day. That was my dream, too. For a young black boy the vision is to become a professional athlete. I had two dreams when I was a child— to be a professional football player and a minister. That was going to be my way out.

My childhood was like many project kids: My mother was single when my older brother and I were born. She didn't marry my stepfather until I was about seven years old. I guess I was lucky in one respect, because I did know my father, and he claimed me as his son even though he never married my mother.

I only weighed six pounds when I was born; however, after three months I weighed in at more than thirty pounds. Incredibly, I caught up with all of my cousins and passed most of them who were two and three years older.

Mom says I also had a unique way of letting her know I was finished with my bottle. She gave me milk in a glass

---

"How in the world could a little guy from the projects in Chattanooga, Tennessee, achieve such a goal, having his name recognized by every football fan in the country? Dreams combined with hard work really do come true."

---

bottle, and when I had my fill, I would throw it up against the wall. So much for glass bottles.

My mother married my stepfather, Leonard Collier, and they moved to Kansas where he was stationed in the Army. My brother Julius and I decided to stay with my grandmother and our other friends in Chattanooga.

My grandmother was a great lady. She took care of us like a mother, which she really was, and taught us right from wrong, based on the Good Book. Mother, as we affectionately called her, took us to an all black church that had a white pastor.

Reverend Ferguson was a fantastic man. He loaded all of us in his van and took us roller skating, on picnics, and to ball games. He taught me an important principle at a very early age: that you show people you love them by spending time with them. Today I mention Reverend Ferguson's name when I speak all over the country. I haven't seen him since I was a kid in Chattanooga, and I sure would like to tell him thanks for caring and showing it.

Those Beautiful Cat Eye Marbles

Another principle I learned in the projects was how to overcome fear. My prize possessions were the most beautiful cat eye marbles known to man. I would do just about anything to keep from losing them—that is, anything except fight the neighborhood bully.

I tried all sorts of street psychology to hold on to my cat eyes. I even gave the guy a few marbles in hopes he would be satisfied. But noooo, he wanted them all. And he usually got what he wanted.

One thing I learned early in life: Fear doesn't disappear by ignoring it or trying to appease it. Fear must be faced head on and dealt with.

As you will discover about me in this book, I do a lot of dreaming. On one particular night I dreamed about the project bully—definitely not my favorite subject. In my dream, I had a brand new set of cat eyes, and he knew about them. As he sauntered up to me, I knew what he wanted and also that I would not give them up.

He demanded my marbles; I told him to forget it—they were staying with me. He drew back his fist to hit me, and much to my pleasure, I hit him back (at this point I *knew* I was dreaming). A fast-hitting scuffle took place, and then I knocked the bully out cold.

When I awoke the next morning, I had renewed confidence in my ability to protect my cat eyes. As I approached the gathering of the project marble holders, I mentally prepared myself for the oncoming conflict.

This wasn't a dream; this was reality. He was already there, and I was ready. He called for my marbles, and I refused. He reached to take them; I mustered all my cour-

---

> **"Then like lightning out of the sky came an instant flash—why not pray and ask God to help me hit a home run? Why not? I stepped out of the batter's box and prayed, believing that He could help me do it."**

---

age, and maybe some stupidity, and punched him in the nose. I don't know if I really hurt him or not, but I got to keep my marbles.

When I think about it now, I don't know what I would have done if I had missed with my swing, and he had cold-cocked me with a right cross and took my cat eyes anyway. All I know is I faced my fear and learned to overcome it.

That's how I am going to remember it anyway.

Pray, Close Your Eyes, and Swing

Another principle I learned was that it doesn't hurt to hope and pray. I was playing Little League baseball and was one of the bigger players on the team. Any guy my size is expected to be a definite threat to hit a home run every turn at bat. Well, my bat and most of those balls never got to know each other. But on one occasion they did.

I was up to bat against a typical Little League pitcher. Based on my batting average, he could have been an excel-

lent pitcher or one of the best pitchers or capable of un-
leashing an unbelievable roundhouse curve. From my perspective, they were all fantastic hurlers. I was waiting him
out to check his control, but his first two pitches were
strikes right down the middle of the plate. I had no choice
but to seriously consider swinging on the next pitch.

Then like lightning out of the sky came an instant
flash—why not pray and ask God to help me hit a home
run? Why not? I stepped out of the batter's box and prayed,
believing that He could help me do it.

I stepped back into the batter's box and prepared to clob-
ber that ball with all my might. I never saw the next pitch,
but I heard and felt my bat connect with the ball. I opened
my eyes just in time to see the ball sailing over the fence.

Now, I know, you may think that the principle I learned
at that game was to pray for anything you want, and God
will give it to you. No way. Prayer doesn't work like that. I
learned never to give up hope. In spite of any circumstance,
never give up hope.

A friend of mine tells the story of a baseball player who
always gave the sign of the cross before he came up to bat.
A priest was sitting in the stands, and another man asked
the priest if making the sign of the cross helped the player
get a hit. The priest replied, "It depends on how good a
hitter he is."

Praying or making the sign of the cross doesn't make
you a better anything, but it does give you hope to do the
best you can.

I was really beginning to love baseball when Dixie
Youth football began in my neighborhood. For lack of anything else constructive (or rather destructive) to do, I started
playing football, too. However, after a couple of years, our
community ran out of money, and we didn't have any or-
ganized sports until I reached junior high school.

They Really Hit in Junior High

When I was in the seventh grade, I remember watching a NFL highlights film featuring O. J. Simpson. Seeing him gyrate and bounce off tacklers really got me excited about playing football. I made two important monumental decisions while viewing that movie: First, I really wanted to play professional football; and second, I wanted to play defense and hit people and not get knocked around like most running backs do.

My football career resumed in junior high and didn't have quite an auspicious beginning. Man, those eighth and ninth graders were big, and when they hit us seventh graders, we hurt. As a matter of fact, they roughed me up so bad that I decided football was for them, and not for Reggie White. I quit.

At one of the games later in the season, however, I caught a glimpse of the respect and adulation football players receive. I determined to give the sport another try. And because of my size, the coach relented and put me back on the team.

Shortly thereafter, I earned the starting center position and began to really enjoy the game. But in the back of my mind, I was chomping at the bit to play defense.

On this same junior high team I met a friend, an incredible athlete named Charles Morgan. I would play football with him all the way through high school and at the University of Tennessee.

Toughness—A Lesson to Be Learned

I excelled in basketball and football, but I met my match at Chattanooga Howard High School. His name was Coach Robert Pulliam.

Coach Pulliam had been a great defensive lineman at the University of Tennessee and seemed to see something inside of me that no one else knew existed. I was a good football player, but I wasn't tough enough to be an excellent player.

One day after a grueling practice, Coach approached me and told me that I could be the best defensive player to ever play the game of football. I was just a sophomore in high school at the time and, boy, did my head swell. What I didn't realize was that with praise comes responsibility.

From that day forward, Coach Pulliam pushed me harder than I deemed I could possibly be pushed. I was to learn the lesson that changed my football career.

Some of us were playing a pickup game of basketball in the gym against the coaches, including Coach Pulliam. Now, one of my biggest weaknesses in football was my lack of toughness. By toughness, I don't mean to be bullish or mean like the guy who took my marbles. Toughness in football is being able to take punishment and holding your frustration inside until such time as you can unleash it on your opponent—within the rules, of course.

Coach Pulliam was about six feet two inches, about two hundred and eighty pounds, and guarding me rather closely. Suddenly, I made a fabulous Dr. J move to the basket. The only problem was my football coach was not going to be beat by a slick move. And this became an excellent occasion to teach me a lesson in toughness.

As I moved toward the basket, he decked me with a forearm that seemed to send my teeth flying through the back of my head. My head felt like major headache number twenty-five, but more than that, my pride was really suffering.

I wobbled back to the locker room, sat down on the floor, and began to cry. A few minutes later, in came Coach Pulliam. Inside, I thought, well, it's about time you came to your senses and apologized to your future defensive player of the universe. Boy, was I ever surprised at what he said.

"If you think I'm going to apologize for busting you in the face, you can forget it," he shouted. So much for my theory.

He continued, "Until you start getting tougher and begin dishing out what you have to, I'm going to keep knocking you around."

Right then and there in that old, dingy, smelly locker room, I made a decision to be the toughest player around.

"Coach Pulliam pushed me harder than I deemed I could possibly be pushed. I was to learn the lesson that changed my football career."

In the next game of basketball, Coach Pulliam guarded me again, and grabbed me, and threw me down on the hardwood. I picked myself up, got right back in his face, and did the same to him, with respect of course. It didn't take too many more wrestling matches with Coach on the basketball court before the teacher finally got through to the student.

I played tight end and defensive end all the way through my high school career. Can you guess which position I enjoyed most? I actually began to hate offense and couldn't wait to hit people on defense. Toughness.

My senior year at Howard I was named football and basketball player of the year in Chattanooga. Believe it or not, I could actually slam dunk a basketball. I also was honored as the "Two-Sport Player of the Year" in the country. Some guy named Patrick Ewing was first runner up in the voting to me. I wonder what ever became of him?

It's Time for College Football!

For a couple of years I had been getting offers from several colleges about playing football for them. My good friend, Charles Morgan, had been receiving letters from colleges since he was in the eighth grade. During our senior year we decided that whatever university we chose to attend, we were going together as roommates.

I had received serious offers from UCLA, Oklahoma, Ohio State, Miami, Alabama, and Michigan. The NCAA (National Collegiate Athletic Association) allows a high school student to visit six schools of his choice at the school's expense. The last college on my list was the University of Tennessee.

The school that impressed me most on my visits was UCLA. I really liked the students' laid-back attitudes. The black athletes were great friends with the whites and Hispanics. Since I grew up in a mixed neighborhood, I really had a good feeling about this school. But California is very far from Tennessee. I went back to Chattanooga, knowing UCLA was just too far from home.

The decision was made for me one Saturday afternoon on a visit to Neyland Stadium in Knoxville, Tennessee. When the Big Orange team hit the field amidst the screams of ninety-six thousand raucous fans, I was awestruck. That settled it. Charles and I were off to play for the Volunteers of Tennessee against the Auburn Tigers, the Alabama Crimson Tide, the Georgia Bulldogs, the Florida Gators—and any other team that dared step onto the same field with them.

Everything was coming up big oranges, until that first day of practice in pads. What a rude welcome to college football.

MY BLOOD
RUNS ORANGE!

Charles Morgan and I arrived in Knoxville on a very warm, muggy day in August, ready to begin our lives as new members of the Big Orange football team. More than forty thousand students and the huge campus overwhelmed us: The University of Tennessee certainly was a whole lot bigger and a whole lot different from Chattanooga Howard High School. Discovering where the football players lived proved a challenge, but we were as excited as any two high school kids could be when we reported to the athletic dorm to receive our room assignment.

You see, Charles and I had been promised that we could room together as part of our incentive for signing with Tennessee. As I mentioned, Charles and I had played ball together since junior high; we were good friends and wanted to continue that friendship as roommates in college. Charles had wanted to go to the University of Miami, but I talked him out of it after we were told we would be sharing the same room.

Now we were in Knoxville, ready to find out what college life was all about. When we walked up to the information desk, however, our hopes were dashed. To our horror, we discovered we were in different rooms. There must be some mistake, I insisted, but there wasn't. Charles and I were separated. To say we were disappointed is more than an understatement. We had counted on this, but somehow it hadn't been communicated through the channels of campus housing. Every room was assigned; no possibility of changing with someone else existed; we'd just have to "room together next year." But to two young, even though big, guys from Chattanooga, it was like losing contact with home, losing a sense of security. As a matter of fact, Charles ended up leaving UT a couple of weeks later and never returned to college. Sometimes I wonder if I should have talked him into coming to UT. He may have gone on to the University of Miami and had a great career. And I will tell you this, if we had been permitted to be roommates that first year, I sincerely believe Charles would have stayed in school.

Regardless, here I was. At six feet five inches, I was recognized by other students as "probably an athlete," and I loved the attention I received. Adjusting to not having Charles as my "roomy" was hard enough. Walking around campus made me feel important, as I experienced the mystique surrounding the members of the football team. But then came my next seemingly insurmountable obstacle— putting on pads and hitting with the real big boys.

Practice—A Hard-Hitting Experience

My size always intimidated other high school football players. Now, when I lined down against the college players, I was the one who was intimidated. These guys were all as big as or even bigger than I had ever hoped to be. Intimidated? There's not strong enough language to use in describing my feelings that first day of practicing in pads. I was gripped with soul-shattering terror. These guys were monsters and appeared more than ready to devour some fresh new meat from high school.

I'm still not sure what got me through that first day of hitting and shoving and verbal abuse, but somehow I survived, learning really fast that I had to demonstrate my toughness just as Coach Pulliam had taught me.

Then my greatest fear—what I had dreaded all the years I played football—materialized one day in practice. Lamont Holt Jeffers was a big, burly, upperclassman and a very experienced linebacker. I was pursuing the ball carrier from

---

"The whole practice field became one humongous spinning top; I was at its center trying desperately to catch hold of something to stop it. My lungs were empty, and every gasp for oxygen came up short."

---

my defensive end position when Lamont accidently blindsided me and buried his helmet in my ribcage. In football terms, I got my bell rung.

Let me make a feeble attempt at describing my feelings very shortly after impact. First, my head felt like somebody reached inside, grabbed my brain, and squeezed it like a sponge, leaving nothing behind capable of thought. I was in a complete daze. My chest felt as if King Kong had placed me in a vise, expending all of his energy to turn the handle one last time, before pouncing on me with all four feet.

The whole practice field became one humongous spinning top; I was at its center trying desperately to catch hold of something to stop it. My lungs were empty, and every gasp for oxygen came up short. As they carried me from the field, I only had one rational thought—get me back to my mamma in Chattanooga.

A few hours later and after many cobwebs had disappeared from my brain, I made a desperate phone call to my mother.

"Thelma, I think I'm going to have to give it up. I just can't take it anymore," I explained.

A wise woman, my mother. After a short pause, my mother spoke, "Reggie, if that's what you want to do, then do it. But remember what you told me before you left for Knoxville."

"What are you talking about?" I asked. Suddenly, my mind went straight as an arrow to the conversation I had had with my mother. I had assured her that as long as God blessed me with the ability to play football, I would expend every ounce of energy in my body doing just that and would never, ever give up!

Thanks a lot, Mom, you really know how to zero in on the truth. Now, I knew there was no way I could quit. I would just have to take what Coach Pulliam had taught me about toughness and hang in there—even if it took *every* ounce of energy I had!

Starting Left Defensive End

I started playing regularly about the second game of the season against the University of Southern California Trojans—O. J. Simpson's alma mater. Southern Cal was known for producing some of the best offensive linemen in the country, but I was fighting them off solidly, which was commendable, especially for a freshman. Skills of a defensive lineman I didn't even know I possessed earned me a starting position at defensive end about the sixth game of that season. That stayed my position throughout my years at Tennessee.

I spent some time in the weight room and on the track during the off-season and increased my strength and endurance substantially. I'm a firm believer in setting goals. If you don't work toward something, you'll end up working for nothing.

No Tennessee Vol football player had won the Southeastern Conference Player of the Year award since my coach, Johnny Majors, had done it in 1956. I wanted to be the next player to do it.

After doing some research, I found out that no defensive player had won the trophy since Georgia's Jake Scott accomplished it in 1968. As any football fan will tell you, quarterbacks and running backs get much more attention and press than defensive players.

So, my mind was set. I'd be the next Tennessee Vol and the next defensive player to win the Southeastern Conference Player of the Year award before I graduated. I was planning on it.

The Old Injury Bug

All I cared about was being an All-American and becoming SEC Player of the Year. I really didn't think about my teammates or the discipline it was going to take to get me there. I was selfish and self-centered with my own goals instead of thinking about the overall big picture, the one that included my whole team. I sincerely believe that because I was so personal-goal oriented, I ended up hurt most of that season.

Before our first game of the season against the Duke University Blue Devils, I sprained my ankle. Then a couple of games later, I sprained my other ankle against the Alabama Crimson Tide. Our victory over the Tide helped to soothe the injury somewhat, but because of our grueling schedule, my ankles never had a reasonable amount of time to properly heal.

Then as if to add insult to injury, I chipped a bone in my elbow. Never say "what else can happen?" because it usually does. And in my case it did—I pinched a nerve in my neck the last game of the season. Physically, I was really hurting, and playing anywhere near my ability, much less up to my expectations, was hard.

Then to make matters worse, articles started appearing in the press implying I just wasn't tough enough. The reason they gave? My religious beliefs! How ridiculous!

Every article I read made me more determined during my senior year to make those writers eat every derogatory remark. I was just plain injured, and my religious faith had nothing to do with it.

I realized that I wanted all the accolades of being the best, but I wasn't willing to pay the price to accomplish it. I had to quit running my mouth and start putting my actions where my mouth was. When I put my convictions into motion, I started becoming what I had talked about.

Time to Get Serious About Lifting and Running

I sat in my room, pondering my performance the past season and realized I needed to work on some areas. The best way to cut down on injuries is by spending more time in the weight room. Weight training was definitely a weak spot; I had not really taken the weight room seriously. When I would ask a teammate if he wanted to lift, he'd refuse and I would agree and do something else, anything except lift weights.

That had to change. I came to the conclusion that if I was going to be the "player of the year," I had to spend

---

"Many coaches try to bulldog you, shame you, or curse at you to motivate you to be a better player. I always hated negative motivation like that."

---

time in the weight room whether I had someone to go with or not.

I continued to invite buddies to go with me, but when they said no, I went anyway. Incredibly, after hearing my invitation and seeing me go without them, many eventually followed my example and began lifting regularly along with me. Isn't that something? When you try to do the right thing, it's amazing how others will eventually join you.

Another area of weakness was in my conditioning. I had to spend a lot more time running on the track to improve my endurance. Here again, my friends saw me doing it, and they started joining me in sprints and laps.

Defensive Coordinator Larry Marmie

When practice started in August for my senior year, I was confident I was as physically ready as I could possibly be. And now my preparation included a new defensive coordinator named Larry Marmie.

Coach Marmie was fantastic—just what I needed. Many coaches try to bulldog you, shame you, or curse at you to motivate you to be a better player. I always hated negative motivation like that.

Coach Marmie was different. The first day of practice he promised us he would never attack us personally when we made mistakes. Yes, he would yell at us, but he stuck by us. He worked with us so closely that I think any one of us would have died for him. If he told us to run around the outside parking lot at Neyland Stadium, we would have done it, because we knew he cared about us and it must be for our good.

As the season progressed, Coach Marmie got moves out of me I never knew I had. He was such an encourager that you had no choice but to do your best. I ended the season with fifteen sacks and more than one hundred tackles.

The previous three years Tennessee had been last in the Southeastern Conference in total defense. By the end of my senior year we had gone from the worst defense to the best defense. Can you guess which coach I feel was the difference?

Head Coach Johnny Majors

My respect for head coach Johnny Majors never wavered. He demanded his players to do it right the first time. He was such a perfectionist about game preparation; we would spend hours preparing for just about any situation that might occur against every opponent on our schedule. During my four-year career at Tennessee, I can't remember one single game when the opposing team showed us in a game something that we weren't ready for. I learned from Coach Majors the importance of preparation—know what your goal is.

During practice Coach Majors liked to walk around, shouting instructions at individual players and coaches. Most people don't see the humorous side of Johnny Majors very much, but every once in a while it shows itself. And you just have to take advantage of it.

At one particular practice, for some reason he remained seated, instead of being his usual self, pacing around the field. We were hard at work, going through some pass protection drills, when one of the guys noticed that Coach Ma-

---

"I learned from Coach Majors the importance of preparation— know what your goal is."

---

jors looked like he was asleep. We told a couple of the assistant coaches, but they told us to keep quiet and ignore him.

Several minutes later he was still sitting with his head down. The horn blasted, signaling the end of practice. Coach Majors was so startled that he jumped to his feet and yelled, "That's the best practice I have ever seen." Right, Coach!

I still today keep in contact with Coach Majors. I wouldn't have learned as much playing for any other head coach, I believe.

One of the best teams we played that year was the Louisiana State University Tigers. The Bayou Bengals featured an All-American running back named Dalton Hilliard, who later played with the New Orleans Saints. I was in their backfield nearly all day.

I still have the film of that game and pull it out every once in a while for old times' sake. Well, I also enjoy looking at it for my ego, too. On one particular play I hit Dalton just as he was receiving the ball in the backfield. It wasn't his fault I beat his timing, but I crunched him so badly that I cringe every time I watch it. It's hard to believe that the kid who didn't know much about toughness could reach the point where he played with such intensity.

Southeastern Conference Player of the Year

My senior year was about as good as a defensive lineman could have. But what made it even better was that the same press corps that criticized me for not being tough enough voted me the "Southeastern Conference Player of the Year." I was also one of the four finalists for the Lombardi Trophy given to the outstanding college lineman of the year. Dean Steinkuhler of Nebraska won it, but, hey, I had already accomplished my goal and more.

I traveled to the Orient to play in the Japan Bowl and then to Hawaii to take part in the Hula Bowl. Playing in the Hula Bowl definitely provided me with the incentive to return to Hawaii for the Pro Bowl a few years later.

I really loved playing for the University of Tennessee Volunteers, and my heart still skips a beat whenever the band strikes up with "Rocky Top." "Good ole Rocky Top, Rocky Top, Tennessee."

One of my best friends and teammates at UT was Willie Gault, now of the L.A. Raiders. We had a lot of great times together and our families are still friends today. Daniesse Gault and Sara have prearranged their daughter Shakari and or Jeremy's wedding!

Then there are the Big Orange fans. These are the most incredible fans found anywhere on the face of the earth. Philadelphia fans are great, but Tennessee fans fill Neyland Stadium ninety-five thousand strong at every single home game, screaming their lungs out, win or lose. Sure, they like to win, but even when you lose, they still love you. I don't think I have ever heard a Tennessee crowd boo a Tennessee team.

Needless to say, if I had it to do over again, I would still choose the Big Orange. There's just no experience in the world like running through the big "T" formed by the band at the beginning of every home game. My body was always covered with chill bumps, my emotions cresting at fever pitch.

My blood runs orange so much that I built a swimming pool at our home outside of Knoxville in the shape of a T. All the weights in my weightroom are, that's right, orange and white.

The USFL or the NFL?

At the end of my college football career, I was chosen in the first round by the Memphis Showboats of the newly formed United States Football League. I was just a few class hours short of finishing my degree, but the Showboats made me an offer I couldn't refuse at the time. However, education is very important to me, and I finished my Bachelor of Science degree in human services in 1990.

A lot of people wondered why I passed up the chance to play in the glamorous National Football League and instead chose to play in the shaky USFL. Well, I really wanted to stay close to home, and I could surely do that by playing with Memphis. I also liked the idea of playing under the Showboats' head coach, Pepper Rogers. I guess the money had something to do with it, too, even though I never received everything since the League ceased to exist at the end of my second season.

Practice with the Showboats started immediately at the conclusion of the college season, and I felt I was ready to begin my pro football career. My dream of becoming a professional football player was finally a reality. The USFL and the Showboats were too good to be true, which providentially also became a reality.

T·H·R·E·E

THE MEMPHIS SHOWBOATS

It's hard for me to describe the great feelings I had after the Memphis Showboats made me their first round pick in the USFL draft of 1984. I would play professional football in my home state, my family and friends would see me play, and most importantly, I convinced my sweetheart, Sara, to marry me before I moved to Memphis.

The USFL was a fantastic place to play football. I had more fun and enjoyment by far while playing there than in the National Football League.

The Memphis Showboats ate together, played football together, spent leisure time together, and almost always included our families in our activities. Sara and I look back on those days with very fond memories and as a time of real family bonding for us. Families were so close that we keep in touch with many of them even today.

Head Coach Pepper Rogers and Others

One of the reasons the Showboats were so laid-back and family oriented was Coach Pepper Rogers. His distinctive style was evident in just about everything he did.

Take, for example, his clothes. The way he mixed and matched stripes, plaids, and paisley would make punk rockers look like Ivy Leaguers. He always looked as though he just got up, grabbed his clothes while still asleep, and looked at them for the first time when he entered the locker room.

Maybe he brushed his teeth, but he never brushed or combed his hair and rarely bothered to put on a pair of socks. We constantly joked with him about how he would never make the cover of *GQ*, but he seemed to thrive on the attention given to his style of dress.

Then one day he came into the locker room before practice and shocked us all. We were getting dressed for a rough practice when the doors flew open and there he stood, dressed like the groom right off the cover of a bridal magazine. He was wearing a black tuxedo, complete with tails, top hat, cane, and shiny black patent shoes. Each stud and cuff link on his shirt was in place; the cummerbund fit perfectly.

Every player was in awe; we couldn't believe our eyes. Then one guy looked closer at his shoes and discovered his socks didn't match his pants, primarily because there were no socks. Coach Rogers, all right. Having a little fun with us, but he just couldn't change all his habits.

Coach Pepper Rogers had a distinct style of football, too. He had his teams play like he dressed: wide open and unpredictable. The opposing teams never knew what to expect from the Showboats.

Another great relationship in Memphis was with my defensive line coach, Chuck Dickerson. I really respect and appreciate Coach Dickerson because he taught me so much about the importance of technique in pass rushing and defensive line play. He knew when to push a man and just how far to get the most out of him. I owe a lot of my success today to Coach Dickerson.

I also cultivated two close friendships while with the Showboats. Walter Lewis and Calvin Clark will never know how much their lives influenced me in Memphis.

Walter had been a quarterback for Tennessee's arch rival, the Alabama Crimson Tide. In spite of my dislike for Alabama (remember—my blood will always run orange), Walter became a true and trusted friend whom I still confide in today. He's now the running back coach for Bill Curry at the University of Kentucky.

Calvin Clark is now the director of the Fellowship of Christian Athletes in Memphis and we get together as often as possible, at least a couple of times each year. We talk on the phone much more than that. We have a lot in common; if it weren't for my wife Sara, Calvin wouldn't have met his wife Devorah.

"Coach Pepper Rogers had a distinct style of football, too. He had his teams play like he dressed: wide open and unpredictable. The opposing teams never knew what to expect."

Sara had often commented on how much of a shame it was that Calvin wasn't married. Of course, she decided to do something about it.

Our friendship with Calvin continued after we moved to Philadelphia, where Sara served as a chaplain in a state mental hospital. She came home one particular evening and calmly announced that she had met Calvin's future wife that day by way of the Holy Spirit. While making the rounds with another chaplain, Reverend Hawkins, she was introduced to a hospital employee named Devorah.

When most women make statements like that, their friends might ignore them or agree without thinking. But whenever my Sara says that, watch out, because it's probably going to come true.

A short time after that eventful meeting, Calvin and Devorah got together in Philadelphia, and a-year-and-a-half later they were married. They now have a son, Joshua Calvin, and are happily married in Memphis today. Devorah's and Sara's love for each other is like no other. I pray that all Christian women would have a fellowship like Dee and Sara. Calvin and Devorah are a large part of our lives. Now we have Joshua Calvin to look forward to.

Let me tell you one thing. If you are single and want to remain that way, stay away from Sara.

Tennessee Recruiting Scandal

While I was playing with the Showboats, a woman reporter whom I considered a friend from my UT days, called me. She asked if I would answer a few questions for a survey about college recruiting. When she asked if I had received money from anyone while playing football at Tennessee, we were supposed to be speaking confidentially. I told her that I had accepted some cash from some friends of our family.

Then she asked if they were alumni of the University of Tennessee. I explained to her that I didn't know for sure, but that they might be.

A few days later a Tennessee newspaper came out with the story: Reggie White received money while at UT from some University of Tennessee alumni. As soon as I heard about the story, I confronted the reporter and asked why she had printed such an article about statements she assured me were made in confidence.

She made some lame excuse. A short time later I found out she had been pressured by her editor to print the story, confidential or not. I also learned that she quit reporting for that particular newspaper very soon after this incident. I guess we still have choices.

Before long the University of Tennessee asked me to sign an affidavit stating that I had not received money from any Tennessee alumni. In retrospect, I should not have signed it, but I did.

Let me set the record straight. I was wrong for signing the affidavit. At the time I believed I had received money

---

"A few days later a Tennessee newspaper came out with the story: Reggie White received money while at UT from some University of Tennessee alumni."

---

from an alumnus and should not have signed anything stating otherwise. Sure, it turns out that what I signed was a true statement. But I didn't realize this when I signed it.

A few years later, I was being interviewed by a magazine reporter from *Sport* magazine, whom I also considered to be a friend. Some people from the University of Tennessee had made some disparaging remarks about me, so I used my mouth to try to get even with my old school. I told him that I had lied when I signed that paper, and that it was time I was honest about it. I knew what I was saying.

Well, you can guess what happened. That's right, everything I said was in the next issue of *Sport*.

A short time later I called that family friend in Chattanooga who had given the money to help with my expenses while at Tennessee. In the course of our conversation I asked him when he graduated from UT. Man, was I surprised at his response. He never attended the University of Tennessee; he was just an avid Vol football fan.

This man had been a friend of our family for more than fourteen years and had helped me financially while I was in school. But he never attended one single class and was definitely not an alumnus.

Now, let me explain why I took money from friends while I was in school. The NCAA (National Collegiate Athletic Association), which is the governing association for college athletics, states that student athletes must not accept any money while they are attending college on an athletic scholarship. The rule also states that a student athlete cannot have a job or receive any remuneration from an employer while he is attending college. Both sound good in principle, but certainly not in practice.

I came from a family that could not afford to provide even the barest essentials for me, such as clothes, laundry, gasoline, social activities, and toiletries like shaving cream and deodorant. I dare say that many student athletes even today are in the same situation.

I wanted to have a job to earn money for these things, but it was against the rules. I sincerely believe that the NCAA really needs to reconsider its thinking on this important matter and come up with some guidelines, maybe even allowances for student athletes to earn needed money honestly.

The Infamous Sock Story

One day during my rookie year with the Showboats, I decided to go to a men's store and do some shopping. I selected several items of clothing there and proceeded to the checkout counter since I was charging the whole lot. I didn't watch closely to see if what was packed was what I actually wanted. I got my boxes and bags and went back to my home.

"The salesman at the store had obviously taken advantage of me and stuffed the extra socks in the bag. Then upon closer examination of my sales receipt, I realized that he had charged me for every pair."

When I started unpacking everything, I noticed that one bag was unusually large. I had picked out just a few pairs of socks, but this particular bag was bulging. As I emptied the sack, I found that there were more than thirty pairs of white tube socks in that bag.

I was furious. The salesman at the store had obviously taken advantage of me and stuffed the extra socks in the bag. Then upon closer examination of my sales receipt, I realized that he had charged me for every pair.

Fuming, I packed up everything I had bought and rushed back to that store. I returned everything that I had bought that day.

A few days later, a newspaper article appeared, detailing the "excessive number of socks" I had bought from a local men's store. The press had a field day.

That particular store became so enamored with the story that they had some "Reggie White" socks made to sell to the Showboat fans in Memphis. Evidently, they did pretty well, because at every home game for the next few weeks whenever I performed well on the field, fans waved these

white tube socks with my name on them all over the stands.
Talk about a store making a good situation out of a bad one.

Drafted by the NFL Eagles

In the Spring of 1985, the Philadelphia Eagles selected me as
their first round choice in the supplemental draft. (I was the
fourth player picked overall.) In the supplemental draft,
NFL teams pick players who were not in the college draft.
Usually these players are graduating early or want to forfeit
their remaining years of college eligibility and start playing
professional football. This particular draft for the most part
was made up of USFL players who wanted to move into
the NFL.

The New York Giants had the first pick and chose Gary
Zimmerman, an offensive lineman that they later traded to
the Minnesota Vikings. I still kid with Giants' coach Bill
Parcells today and tell him how I am going to make life
miserable for him every game we play them, because he
had the chance to get me and blew it!

The Eagles like to remind me of how much money they
paid to buy my contract from the Showboats. Well, they
also have to remember that I too gave up a lot of money to
sign with the Eagles and thus forfeit my contract with the
Showboats.

However, signing with the Philadelphia Eagles proved to
be providential. The United States Football League folded
when they "won" their lawsuit against the National Football
League and received the ridiculous judgment of one dollar.

The NFL was a completely different breed of football
from the USFL. The players were bigger, faster, and cockier
than I could ever have imagined.

THE LIFE
OF AN NFL
PLAYER

I joined the Eagles after the fourth game of the season, and one of the first things I knew I needed to do was find a good friend on the team. That first day in practice I met Tom Struthers, and we immediately became close friends. Two weeks later he was released by the team. Here today, gone tomorrow.

One of the toughest situations in developing friendships in the NFL is when those friends get traded or cut from the team. The trades or cuts come without any warning. One day you are best friends; the next day he's gone to another city.

So then I developed a great friendship with two other guys, Cedrick Brown and Alan Reid. They were both only about five feet eight inches tall, and when we appeared together, we looked like Mutt and two Jeffs. The next year they got cut. I thought, "Oh no, here we go again."

At this time I met Keith Byars. Keith and I became instant great friends. Keith is humble, which is a rare commodity in the NFL, and is always quick to encourage me and his teammates, especially when we need it most.

Even though I missed the first four games of the season, I still was voted the Defensive Rookie of the Year by my fellow NFL players. I also made the first team NFL All-Rookie Team and Honorable Mention All-Pro.

For the next few years as a Philadelphia Eagle, I was fortunate in being elected to the Pro Bowl every year in the NFL, as well as being on the All-Madden Team each year. I guess you have to be big and tough to make "Big John" Madden's team, because the trophy he gives you is a solid piece of rock weighing about forty pounds.

Buddy Ryan

When I joined the Eagles in 1985, the head coach was Marion Campbell. We had a so-so year, so at the end of the season, Coach Campbell was dumped and the Eagles hired Buddy Ryan. Coach Ryan had been the defensive coordinator with the Chicago Bears and was a driving force in the Bears' world championship season the previous year.

I had heard many great things about Buddy from my good friend Mike Singletary, the outstanding linebacker with Chicago. He felt that Buddy was a real friend to the players, so I couldn't wait to get started playing under Buddy Ryan.

Then came that first day of practice. It was about ninety degrees in the middle of August. I mean it was hot! And you know hot isn't so bad, except when it's humid. And it was humid! And then, to top it all, here was a new coach that needed to make the right first impression on his new football team. And did he ever make a lasting first impression.

I thought he was going to kill us. First we ran, then we hit, then we ran, then we hit, then we ran some more, and then we hit some more. Then when we thought everything was over, he made us run a few more sprints. I personally thought that he was mad, that he might have a vendetta against us.

We found out later that there was a definite method to his madness. Coach Ryan just wanted to weed out the guys who couldn't take hard work and diligent training. If they couldn't do it during practice, they certainly couldn't do it during the games.

Some starters were cut or traded because they couldn't fit into his system. I was really quite surprised at some of these moves, but, hey, he was the head coach.

Then at one point during that first day of practice, he said something to me that blew me away. Coach Ryan told me that I was the best defensive lineman he had ever seen.

"I guess you have to be big and tough to make 'Big John'Madden's team, because the trophy he gives you is a solid piece of rock weighing about forty pounds."

I thought to myself, "Wait a minute, Reggie, this guy hasn't even seen you go through a complete practice. And he's saying you are the best defensive lineman in the league. Whoa!"

Buddy Ryan had coached Carl Eller, Richard Dent, and Dan Hampton, just to name a few excellent Hall-of-Fame and All-Pro defensive linemen. And he's saying I'm the best of these guys. I didn't know if he was trying to motivate or intimidate me, but I chose to believe him and worked as I had never worked for any other coach before.

I worked harder that preseason than in any other in my whole football career. If Coach Ryan said that to motivate me, it worked.

Buddy Ryan also became a father figure to many guys on the Eagles. As one of my teammates, Kenny Jackson, told me, Buddy was a father figure most to the players who grew up without fathers, predominantly the black players like me. We were closer to Buddy than the other guys were, and I think you can understand why. Although it took a couple of years for him to get the team players he wanted, when he did, he treated them like real men, and he treated some of us like sons. My relationship to Buddy and his wife Joani has been more than a professional relationship. We enjoy them so much. They are sincere, loving, kind, and caring, and a joy to be around. We have already missed them. We just want the world to know that Sara and I love them with all our hearts.

Something which gained him respect from his players happened during the NFL players strike. Buddy knew that he would be coaching us for a long time after that strike was over. So he supported us *as players* during the strike as no other coach in the NFL even attempted. I don't believe the Eagles' management ever forgave him for his player support during that time. Even today I can't understand why the Eagles' front office couldn't see how much he was helping us and the team at the same time.

I never forget Coach saying, "When you go out, you go out together. When you come back, you come back together." Every single Eagles player who had doubts about liking Buddy Ryan subsequently became his staunchest supporter during that strike.

A Team Effort

What we accomplished and what we fell short of as a team were not the complete responsibility of Buddy Ryan. We won as a team and we lost as a team, and this was not because of the way Buddy Ryan coached alone. Buddy and his staff always had us prepared to win every game we stepped onto the field to play.

I remember during the 1990 season game against the Washington Redskins. We were playing at home before our own beautiful fans, and we were ready to demolish the 'Skins again, just as we had in the previous meeting during the regular season.

We were really struggling, especially on offense, and our quarterback, Randall Cunningham, just wasn't getting the job done. We were down by one touchdown in the third quarter, even though everybody knew that Randall could break it for six points on any play. But he wasn't into the flow of the game, and Buddy pulled him, All-Pro and everything else, and replaced him with our backup quarterback, Jim McMahon.

People may say, "You don't bench an All-Pro quarterback, regardless of how bad a day he's having." However, Buddy cared more about the team than he did about a player's pride. Randall wasn't upset with Buddy; he knew something needed to be done and maybe that would do it. Well, it didn't, and we went on to lose another game we had been picked to win and very well should have. The loss wasn't Coach Ryan's fault; it was the team's fault!

Buddy had taken us to three straight playoffs—more than enough to remain as head coach on any team in the NFL. But not the Eagles. As the old saying goes, "When things aren't going right, fire the coach."

Even so, when I heard on the radio that Buddy had been fired, I was really surprised. The man certainly deserved better.

I sincerely believe that if Buddy Ryan had had all his key players going into each training camp, instead of always having some holding out because of contract disputes with management, we would have three Super Bowl titles under our belts. I wish the Eagles' management could shoulder some of the responsibility themselves for not giving Buddy the chance to have all his starters at the beginning of each preseason.

Coach Ryan never had the opportunity to use all of his top players the first day of training camp. And anybody with any professional football sense knows that has to hurt you for the whole season—not just the first few games.

People ask why Buddy never got us past the first round of the playoffs. The reason wasn't Buddy; it was the team. The last two years we thought we were ready, but to be honest, all of us weren't. Some of us had our heads in places other than the football game. It's really amazing how the guys who aren't mentally prepared for battle can pull even the men who are ready right down the tubes with them.

Buddy Ryan brought enthusiasm, intensity, and downright fun to the Philadelphia Eagles. He installed an attack-style defense that always had our opponents wondering what was going to hit them next. The Philadelphia Eagles are a better team today because Buddy Ryan was here.

Our new head coach, Rich Kotite, was Buddy's offensive coordinator. Coach Kotite is an excellent motivator who demands that football be played the right way. It will certainly be different playing under him, but I have no doubt that he'll do a great job and keep us on the winning track. Since I'm talking about Buddy, Rich, and the NFL, I must not forget my defensive line coach, Dale Haupt.

Dale has helped me a great deal in defining my ability as a football player. He has helped me dig deep down inside when the enthusiasm was not there. He's a man I respect and love a great deal. He is the type of coach that makes you want to strangle him one day but give him a hug the next. His wife is quite a beautiful character too.

A Typical Week

Most fans have no idea how a typical week during the football season progresses. Other teams may vary their schedules, but here's how my week is usually spent:

Monday—I roll out of bed to be ready for weightlifting at 10:00 A.M. If we played on artificial turf the day before, I am especially sore. I always feel better after we have played on natural grass. Artificial turf is just a thin layer of rubber covering over concrete. It can wreak havoc on a man's whole body. At about 11:00 A.M. the team looks at game

---

"Buddy Ryan brought enthusiasm, intensity, and downright fun to the Philadelphia Eagles. He installed an attack-style defense that always had our opponents wondering what was going to hit them next."

---

films to see what we did right and what we need to correct from the previous game. Then we go out to the field for some running. Later that night is my radio talk show.

Tuesday—We usually have this day off so I spend the day with my children, Jeremy and Jecolia. Sometimes I even take Sara to the movies as this is one of the few places where I don't have to sign too many autographs.

Wednesday—Special teams come in for practice at 9:00 A.M. I'm not on any special teams, so I usually arrive about 9:30 A.M. and begin watching films of our upcoming opponent. We study the films to analyze how a team uses different formations in different situations. We look for a pattern of certain plays run from formations on second down and long or third down and short yardage. We look for any consistency in the plays that might give us an idea of what we may expect. We look at their players' head movements, their eyes, and their movement on a given play. For example, if their line players are heavyweights, the team will favor a run because each lineman wants to be able to fire out and make his block. If an opponent doesn't have much weight, he may be getting ready for a sweep or even preparing to retreat for pass protection. This practice usually lasts until 4:30 to 5:00 P.M.

Thursday—Usually we run about the same practice schedule as on Wednesday.

Friday—We look at film again, but we have a much shorter practice session.

Saturday—After a short period of looking at films, we practice offensive and defensive schemes for about thirty to forty-five minutes. Then whether we're playing at home or away, we go to the hotel where we will spend the night. While at the hotel, we again look at game film and the coach usually gives a pep talk. After this we usually hold our chapel service since attending church on Sunday morning is impossible. Then it's usually time for bed, because we almost always have an 11:00 P.M. curfew before a game.

Sunday/Gameday—When we are in Philly, I get up early so I can go out to my house to visit with my family. I have to be back at the stadium by 11:00 A.M. to start getting dressed for the game.

After I get to the locker room, I put on shorts and a T-shirt and get my ankles taped. Then I put my pants, pads, and shoes on. I usually put on my regular turf shoes and go out and see what condition the field is in. If it has been raining and the field is still wet, I come back in and put on my rain turf shoes. These shoes have longer cleats and allow my shoes to dig in deeper for better traction. If I were to wear these rain turf shoes on a dry field, I could literally tear up my knee or sustain some other leg injury. Believe it or not, the right shoes are very important to a football player's performance, as well as his well-being.

When I'm on the field before the game starts, I sometimes get the privilege of talking to some of the players from the other teams. Talking to guys like the Redskins' Darrell Green, who has a much higher calling (I'll talk about this in a later chapter) than professional football, really puts this game into perspective.

When the rest of my team comes out onto the field, I put my helmet on and we warm up for the game by exercising and running. We run through some basic offense and de-

---

"Since my son Jeremy turned four years old, the Eagles' staff has allowed him to come to the locker room with me after the game. He stands by my locker and keeps all the other players in stitches by imitating his dad."

---

fense patterns and then head back to the locker room for our last visit there before halftime. Guess where the main traffic jam is—that's right, the rest room!

Now we just sit around and wait to go back out for the start of the game. Well, most of us sit around, except for Reggie Singletary, who paces up and down the aisles of the locker room, shouting and screaming to get everybody motivated and ready to do battle. Sometimes, Byron Evans and Jerome Brown will join Reggie and really get the team going. Now we're ready to leave the locker room and run through the tunnel for the introduction of the starting lineups.

Halftime—We come in from the field, listen to the coaches, use the rest room, and get fired up all over again.

Post Game—When the final gun sounds, I immediately start looking for Sara and the children. Sometimes I see them and other times I can't find them because of all the chaos at the end of a game. Since my son Jeremy turned four years old, the Eagles' staff has allowed him to come to the locker room with me after the game. He stands by my locker and keeps all the other players in stitches by imitating his dad. He's pretty good, too!

My daughter, Jecolia, still doesn't understand why she isn't allowed to enter the locker room, but she has learned to be content when her dad tells her she has to stay with her mother. She gently responds by saying, "OK, Daddy," and it really tears me up inside. I really try to make up for lost time by spending more time with her after we leave the locker room and head for home.

Respected Opponents and Teammates

Some fans ask me who is the best NFL offensive lineman I have to go against. Well, there is not one particular lineman I would identify. But the offensive line of the Washington Redskins is the toughest I have ever played against. They use more people blocking against me, which often causes me great frustration throughout the course of a game.

Two offensive linemen whom I believe are the best I have personally faced are the Miami Dolphins' Dwight Stevenson and the Minnesota Vikings' Ed White.

I'll never forget my first encounter with Ed White. At that time he was thirty-eight years old and finishing up his career with the San Diego Chargers; I was a rookie. I lined down in front of him, envisioning how I was going to blow this old man away.

The ball was snapped; I charged at him with everything I had. Bam! I thought I had hit a solid brick wall. He was so strong and knew exactly how to distribute his weight to receive the greatest amount of impact. I was impressed!

Another offensive tackle whom I believe to be one of the best, although I have never played against him, is Anthony Munoz of the Cincinnati Bengals. Some other good friends and great football players whom I really respect are the Chicago Bears' Mike Singletary and the Detroit Lions' Barry Sanders. These two men also know how to keep professional football in perspective.

Fellow Eagles Al Harris and Todd Bell have really encouraged me. They especially helped me the year I held out signing my contract with the Eagles. They were with the Chicago Bears then and did not sign their contracts the same year the Bears won the Super Bowl. It must have been difficult doing what they believed so strongly in when it meant not being able to play in the game that every player dreams about.

Some other guys I really appreciated in the early days with the Eagles were Roynell Young, Matt Darwin, and Ron Johnson. Roynell was a great friend who had never experienced a character like me. He was real laid-back, and I have always been just the opposite. He didn't quite know how to take me and my wide-open attitude. When he finally left football, I felt as if I had lost a brother. Matt and Ron were sincere brothers as well as good players. Because of their injuries they finally had to retire. I will miss their fellowship.

Keith Byars is a young man I have a lot of respect for, mainly because faith and walk with the Lord. He is one of the most honest people I have ever met. Besides that, he is an outstanding football player. He joins me in taking a firm stand to be a role model of Jesus.

Keith Jackson and Mike Quick are two other guys I am thankful for. They are genuine athletes and outstanding men whom I count as true friends.

Keith Jackson is one of the best tight ends in football. He cares about his teammates on and off the field. Mike Quick, like myself, is a man of principle; however, we express ourselves differently. Mike is a very soft-spoken man. If he believes in something, he quickly stands behind his belief; on the other hand, I am very vocal concerning my beliefs.

And then there is my compadre, Jerome Brown. Most people only know Jerome as wild, crazy, and off-the-wall. But I know when the chips are down, Jerome can be counted upon to come through when you need him most.

PART ✦ TWO

FAITH

HERE COMES JESUS!

Few people in this world would enjoy suiting up in twenty-five pounds of equipment and then running onto a field when the temperature is one hundred degrees plus. I say one hundred degrees plus, because in the dead of summer when you play on astro turf, that plastic grass usually increases the temperature by about ten to fifteen degrees.

In about thirty seconds you start sweating, and in five minutes your uniform is soaking wet with your own body fluids. There isn't enough deodorant in the world to take away the distinct odor of a football team hard at practice in the dog days of summer.

On just such a day in Detroit, we were in a controlled scrimmage against the Lions. In a controlled scrimmage, the coaches schedule the defenses they want their team to run against the opposing offense and the offense they want to pit against the other defense. There are no downs; the offense may run ten to fifteen plays before the other defense gets to leave the field. No turnovers, no downs, no touchdowns: the coaches call the shots.

He's Coming Soon

About an hour and a half into the scrimmage, our defense had been on the field for about ten plays. Both teams were a little testy when we lined up again to practice our pass rush against the Lions' pass protection.

I had been up against a Detroit rookie for most of the day from my left defensive end position and was really able to outmaneuver just about any move he made to stop me. I could tell how frustrated he was when the head gear on our helmets locked us together. Now, instead of helping each other get untangled like grown men, a football player sometimes must show how tough he is by using foul language or outshoving his adversary.

This veteran used language that I would not let my dogs hear. There's something you have to understand here about Reggie White. I can take getting manhandled or beat up. I can even take losing a close game. But I cannot tolerate being cussed out to my face by anybody. To this day I am not sure why I said what I said to this guy after we jerked our helmets apart.

I looked him right in the eye and pointed my finger at his nose and announced, "Jesus is coming back soon, and I hope you're ready." I think the rookie was as shocked at what he heard as I was about what I had said.

I'm sure this guy had been taught as I was all the way from junior high football to never let the opposition suspect you might be intimidated. So like most gridiron performers, he tossed more choice words into my face and returned to his huddle.

After this second barrage of profanity, I was absolutely livid with anger, refusing to return to my own huddle. Instead, I shouted across the field at him, "Jesus is coming back soon, and I hope you're ready."

By this time a few teammates were urging me to our defensive huddle, so I took a few steps backwards to my usual place. The Eagles' huddle formation has the linemen with their backs toward the football, the linebackers facing us, and the cornerbacks and safeties rounding out the corners.

However, instead of facing my teammates, I eyeballed this rookie, as I shouted to my teammates, "Jesus is coming back soon, and I hope he's ready."

Few fans are at most scrimmages, mainly just the two opposing teams, their coaches, trainers, and other team per-

---

"This veteran used language that I would not let my dogs hear. There's something you have to understand here about Reggie White. I can take getting manhandled or beat up. I can even take losing a close game. But I cannot tolerate being cussed out to my face by anybody."

---

sonnel. By now, though, every person on the whole football field was deathly quiet as I shouted to the rookie once again, "Jesus is coming back soon, and I hope you're ready."

The Lions broke their huddle and returned to the line of scrimmage. I made sure I lined down in front of this same rookie and again, I locked eyes with him and deliberately stated, "Jesus is coming back soon, and *I don't think you're ready.*"

Our eyes never wavered. The quarterback started his cadence, calling out several numbers and colors. My eyes focused on my opponent's face, until with my peripheral vision I saw the ball snapped to the quarterback. Then with an ominous confidence, I declared to that rookie, "Here comes Jesus!"

Like a cat pouncing on its prey, I thrust my entire two-hundred and eighty-five pound body right into his chest and drove him back about five yards. He came to rest on his haunches, just in time to witness my destruction of his quarterback. My teammates and Coach Ryan loved this incident so much that, even during games today, they still ask me if Jesus is coming back on the next play.

I Hope You're Ready

It's still quite hard to explain my reason for my actions on that steamy day in Detroit. I wasn't trying to embarrass this guy, and I wasn't trying to show off my strength and prowess as a football player. As a matter of fact, I'm not sure I was completely conscious of my behavior at the time.

Maybe it was the heat. Maybe it was his language. Maybe it was just that my desire to live my life glorifying Jesus Christ permeates my whole being.

Vocalizing my relationship with Jesus Christ is as natural as breathing for me. And I use the word *relationship*, because it's a day-by-day, night-by-night, ongoing communication between Jesus and me. We talk about the blessings as well as the unanswered questions that occur daily in my life.

I'm not saying that any person can use the name of Jesus and beat every opponent. If that were true, I could skip all my practices, forget about my weight training and conditioning, and just concentrate on using different names for Jesus.

I also have to be honest with you and admit that I get beat on some plays and many times don't come close to sacking the quarterback or even making the tackle. But as the old saying goes, "I'm not perfect, but as a believer in Jesus Christ, I am forgiven." Because of that belief, I can forget about my failures and focus on perfecting my successes.

A couple of years ago, we played the Chicago Bears at Soldier Field on a cold September Sunday and lost an important game 13-10. Needless to say, it was a very disappointing loss, and as I sat at my locker getting undressed, I dreaded having to answer questions from the press. I just wanted to take my shower, put my clothes on, get out of Chicago, and hurry back to my family in Philadelphia.

The truth is, it's when you don't want to talk that the others want to talk to you the most. I had just removed my jersey when six reporters walked up, their tape recorders already running.

"How do you feel about the game, Reggie?"

Great question. Sometimes I wonder what they would have thought if I had responded that I was glad the Bears

---

"I didn't state that 'Jesus is Lord,' as some wise religious expression. I simply wanted them to know that, sure I hate losing, but this one game wasn't the end of the world for Reggie White."

---

won because I had a great fishing trip planned and really detested the idea of winning another game that would take us a step closer toward the dumb old Super Bowl.

Instead, I reflected on the game for a few seconds, then looked up from my stool, and replied, "Well, Jesus is still Lord."

All six reporters immediately clicked off their recorders and started to walk away, looking for something more quotable from another player.

As they turned away, I exclaimed, "That's exactly what the devil does when he hears Jesus' name." At this remark, those same reporters returned to my dressing area and listened intently as I explained why I said, "Jesus is still Lord."

I didn't state that "Jesus is Lord," as some wise religious expression. I simply wanted them to know that, sure I hate losing, but this one game wasn't the end of the world for Reggie White. There is so much more than football, such as life as a happy family. Certainly, I had played my heart out to win so we could continue in the playoffs and on to the Super Bowl. But regardless of what happens in our every-day lives—good and, yes, even the bad—Jesus Christ is still Lord, and nothing that occurs on this earth can change that.

I also told those members of the press that they needed me a whole lot more than I needed them. They agreed and since that day, most of the reporters print what I have to say about my relationship with Jesus as much as they do my thoughts on the day's football action.

I want to live and breathe Jesus Christ so much that when people come into contact with me, they see Jesus. I still mess up and fall far short of imitating Him in my life, but He always forgives me and encourages me in my daily walk with Him. When I'm working and when I'm relaxing, with my teammates and with my family, I want my rela-tionship with Jesus to be obvious.

In these next few chapters I'll explain what this relation-ship with Jesus is all about. Using different pass rushing and tackling techniques I practice regularly, I'll parallel them to my daily experience with Him. I'll also tell you more about my family and friends and how God uses them and others to keep me accountable.

If this sounds intriguing to you, read on. If you don't think you are interested, try reading on anyway! I sure would love to share with you what makes Reggie White, Reggie White.

I'll tell you what I told that rookie: *Here comes Jesus!*

TRAINING CAMP CHRISTIANS

Two football players whom I really respect for their skills and desire are Walter Payton and Howie Long. Walter Payton had several fine record-setting seasons as an outstanding running back with the Chicago Bears. Howie Long has excelled as well as a defensive lineman for the Oakland and L. A. Raiders.

What I appreciate most about Walter and Howie is the fact that they are complete football players. Walter Payton runs the ball with more moves and acceleration than few running backs ever have or ever will. But even when he wasn't the focus of attention as the runner, he was just as diligent as a blocker for a teammate as they ran the ball.

He put just as much emphasis on blocking for others as he did on himself when he had the ball. And if Walter Payton spilled his guts out blocking for you, how much would you expend blocking for him?

Howie Long is an excellent pass rusher. He's big and strong with cat-like moves which get him past an offensive lineman and into the backfield putting pressure on the quarterback; many times Howie sacks him. Howie Long is not only a good pass rusher; he also plays as hard against the run as he does against the pass.

Most defensive linemen are either good against the run or good pass rushers. Very few equally dominate rushing the passer as stopping the run. Many teams will substitute different defensive linemen according to the particular game situation, such as an obvious passing down or a short yardage need.

I also work hard at controlling the line of scrimmage from my position whether charging the quarterback or halt-

ing the ball carrier. I enjoy playing defensive end and am so
confident in my abilities that I want every play to come my
way so I can get personally involved in stopping it.

Why am I so confident? Because I work diligently on
being a complete defensive end by practicing pass rushing
techniques, as well as methods for shedding my blockers
and halting the runner.

One of my biggest pet peeves as a Christian professional
football player is a yearly invasion of training camp Christians. These rookies come to camp during preseason in
hopes of making the Eagles and becoming NFL football
players. They are looking for any easy way—not the commitment that a complete football player makes.

Most of these guys will try anything to enhance their
chances, including attending all the Bible studies and any
"religious" function available. Some are not sure there really is a God, but if there might be, they'll even try Him—
anything to make the team.

Maybe it's a promise to start going to church, to give a
large sum of money, or even to give their lives to Him—
anything, just to become a professional football player.
Many athletes sustaining possible career-ending injuries
have also made promises to God that if only He will heal
them so they resume playing, then they will do anything
for Him. Then when God answers their prayers and re-
stores them to health, the vows are forgotten and their previous way of life returns.

Broken Promises to God

First of all, let's get one term straight. Religion. I don't have
"religion," because religion is man's search for God. I'm not
searching for God; I found Him through my relationship
with His Son, Jesus Christ.

Now let's talk about making promises and vows to God if only He will help you. When things are tough, it's easy to make a promise to get out of a jam. But if you are serious, you'll keep your promise and I'll explain why.

In the Old Testament Joshua was about to enter the Promised Land, Canaan. He was told that his wells would

---

"I don't have 'religion,' because religion is man's search for God. I'm not searching for God; I found Him through my relationship with His Son, Jesus Christ."

---

already be dug, his buildings built, and his cattle grazing. What more could Joshua ask for? And then Moses, his mentor, reminded him:

> Be careful that you do not forget the LORD, who brought you out of Egypt, out of the land of slavery. Fear the LORD your God, serve him only and take your oaths in his name. Do not follow other gods, the gods of the peoples around you; for the LORD your God, who is among you, is a jealous God and his anger will burn against you, and he will destroy you from the face of the land. Do not test the LORD your God. (Deuteronomy 6:12–16)

I've seen too many professional football players and even some so-called superstars, who have made commitments to God to get what they think they want. God allowed them to have it, and then they turned their back on Him.

What does God do when you make a promise and then break it? Will He come down on those who use Him just to

satisfy their own needs? I'm not so sure. If you take what
He says in Scripture, His anger will burn against you. I
don't want the God of the universe to have His anger burn-
ing against me, so I'm going to be careful of what promises
I make to Him.

What if you made a promise to Him which you didn't
keep, but you realize now you are wrong and want to start
keeping your vow? Well, I'm happy to say that I serve a
loving God who will forgive you of anything you ask of
Him, if you truly repent.

Let's look at what it means to repent. Repentance means
that you are sorry for your wrongdoings and will try to
make an about-face from your disobedience. Many people
are sorry for their errors, but they don't repent—turn in the
opposite direction. They admit they're wrong, but then go
right back to the wrong behavior. You must do more than
be sorry. As Paul told the Corinthians:

> Yet now I am happy, not because you were made sorry,
> but because your sorrow led you to repentance. For you
> became sorrowful as God intended and so were not
> harmed in any way by us. Godly sorrow brings repen-
> tance that leads to salvation and leaves no regret, but
> worldly sorrow brings death. See what this godly sorrow
> has produced in you: what earnestness, what eagerness to
> clear yourselves, what indignation, what alarm, what
> longing, what concern, what readiness to see justice done.
> At every point you have proved yourselves to be innocent
> in this matter. (2 Corinthians 7:9–11)

Counting the Cost Before You Promise

Another problem training camp Christians encounter is not
counting the cost before they make a promise to God. They
never considered the fact that making a commitment to
Jesus Christ is much more important than making a football

"I've seen too many professional football players and even some so-called superstars, who have made commitments to God to get what they think they want. God allowed them to have it, and then they turned their back on Him."

team. It's like getting into your car to make a four-hundred-mile trip without checking your gas gauge to determine if you need to fill up. Jesus warned His disciples:

> Suppose one of you wants to build a tower. Will he not first sit down and estimate the cost to see if he has enough money to complete it? For if he lays the foundation and is not able to finish it, everyone who sees it will ridicule him, saying, "This fellow began to build and was not able to finish." Or suppose a king is about to go to war against another king. Will he not first sit down and consider whether he is able with ten thousand men to oppose the one coming against him with twenty thousand? If he is not able, he will send a delegation while the other is still a long way off and will ask for terms of peace. In the same way, any of you who does not give up everything he has cannot be my disciple. (Luke 14:28–33)

When you play for an NFL team, you are committed to help your team defeat every opposing team on your schedule. To make that commitment without counting the cost would be like trying to play the New York Giants without studying the films of their previous games. NFL teams change personnel and change offensive and defensive formations on a weekly basis. If you don't study films, you are not committed to winning.

Every time I read that section in Luke, I get excited and challenged all over again. I ask myself if I am willing to give up my arrogance, my pride, my money, my football career, and even my family. Some heavy-duty thinking has to take place before you make a commitment that includes such sacrifices.

Some may say, that's a lot to give up. God doesn't ask you to give it back to Him; He just wants us to realize that everything *belongs* to Him and is there for your enjoyment. The prophet Jeremiah understood when God said:

> "For I know the plans I have for you," declares the LORD, "plans to prosper you and not to harm you, plans to give you hope and a future. Then you will call upon me and come and pray to me, and I will listen to you. You will seek me and find me when you seek me with all your heart." (Jeremiah 29:11–13)

You cannot be a complete human being without filling the spiritual void that is inside every person. Training camp Christians try to fill that void with religion, money, success, sex, drugs, and the list could go on and on. This void can only be filled with a relationship and continued walking with God through His Son, Jesus Christ.

A well-known national television talk-show host once invited a minister of the Gospel on his program. To win the sympathy of the TV audience, he tried to embarrass the minister with question after question. To the talk-show host's chagrin, the minister never gave one answer or opinion of his own. He only quoted Scripture.

At one point the talk-show host asked the man of God why Christians were so narrrow-minded in thinking that they were the only people in the whole world who knew God and who knew they were going to heaven.

> **"You cannot be a complete human being without filling the spiritual void that is inside every person. Training camp Christians try to fill that void with religion, money, success, sex, drugs, and the list could go on and on."**

The minister again quoted Scripture, this time from the New Testament:

I am the way and the truth and the life. No one comes to the Father except through me. (John 14:6)

The preacher then stated, "I didn't say that, God did. If you don't agree with it, tell Him, not me."

And that's the answer for training camp Christians also. The promises made, but not kept; the functions attended, but not experienced; the hopes dreamed, but not put into action—commitment matters. There is no success for a football player—or a Christian—without it.

STANDING FIRM
IN THE TRENCHES

A seismograph can measure the earth's movement. A stopwatch can gauge speed. But nothing comes close to measuring the amount of energy expended when an offensive and a defensive line unleash their power on the other in the trenches of the NFL. Talk about impact!

Television cameras give us a view of just about every angle on a football field. One camera position that the networks have avoided is on the ground looking up into the eyes and forearms and legs of linemen before and during each play. Of course, I guess it would be hard to find a cameraman willing to risk his life lying on the ground between opposing lines to catch just such a picture. But would football fans ever get their eyes and ears full!

Trench play, that area of battle between two lines of antagonistic football teams, is a game of its own within a football game. Until recent years you didn't hear much about line play during a game. Fans are usually told about the quarterback's beautiful spiral passes, the receivers' acrobatic catches, or the scintillating moves of the running backs.

When an offensive line and a defensive line clash, it's not a picture of great beauty. You will hear a lot of groaning, grunting, and "talking," with several choice words you wouldn't repeat to your mother. Brute strength against brute strength—that's what line play is in the NFL. Well, I would like to think there is a little finesse thrown in here and there, from a defensive lineman's point of view. Offensive linemen, on the other hand, have no finesse whatsoever. Their only goal is to bury their man dead or alive—any way it takes to do it! Of course, I may be prejudiced.

I was at a Fellowship of Christian Athletes (FCA) banquet in Nashville, Tennessee, recently when Art Demas, a sixteen-year NFL veteran official, was introduced. Since I, a veteran defensive lineman, was present, he said he wanted to give a new interpretation of holding, adapted for the new season. First, there must be definite evidence of strangulation; second, there must be a definite show of recently drawn blood; and third, if either of these is not shown, you can present a sworn affidavit signed by at least two other interested parties. Now that sounds a little far-fetched, but sometimes I feel that it's not far from the truth.

A Defensive Lineman's Problems

A defensive lineman has to constantly contend with three main problems. These are being blindsided, watching for crackback blocks, and fighting off being double- or triple-teamed. On the football field, I only get angry about two situations, however: when a player curses at me or when an opposing player cheats by holding me or using an illegal block.

First, let's look at what it is to be blindsided. Most football fans have seen quarterbacks get blindsided at one time or another, since of all the players on the field, quarterbacks are most likely to experience this. When a quarterback goes back to pass the ball, he usually turns his back to one side of the field and cannot see anything coming at him from behind. That area is called his blind side.

Let me go on record right now that I never go after a quarterback from his blind side, or head on for that matter, with the intention of hurting him. My job is to keep him from completing the pass or, even better, to sack him so that his team also loses yardage. My goal is never to put an opposing player out of the game.

Other players also run the risk of being blindsided. After the quarterback, the most susceptible positions are on defense. When the ball is snapped, a defensive player positions himself to make a tackle. When he is moving in for the kill, many times his complete attention is on the man with

---

"Trench play, that area of battle between two lines of antagonistic football teams, is a game of its own within a football game."

---

the ball, and he is completely oblivious to any blocker about to lower the boom on him. This is an offensive lineman's dream.

The feeling is like smiling at your best friend, being very much off-guard, and then having him hit you square in the face. However, being blindsided on the football field is probably a little worse because you are anticipating making contact as the "hitter," and in an instant you become the "hittee."

Another potentially crippling injury can occur when the opposing team member performs a "crackback" block on you. This happens when an offensive receiver goes in motion behind the quarterback, toward the opposite side of the field as if he is going to run a pass pattern. Some defensive linemen would think they can forget about that receiver because he is out of sight. No way!

The receiver you thought was out somewhere on a pass pattern stops in his tracks behind the line of scrimmage and blindsides a defensive lineman to oblivion. Crackback blocks can result in very serious injury and could even end a football player's career in a split second. It is legal and the crackback block happens frequently.

Most fans will tell you that when a defensive lineman is double-teamed or triple-teamed, he must really be an outstanding football player. Well, outstanding or not, no one enjoys taking on two or three blockers instead of just one. It happens frequently to me, but I don't think I will ever get to the point that I look forward to it.

I just have to fight twice as hard to get through my blocks and take solace in the fact that one of my teammates, who only has one blocker, will break through and make the play. Whether I make the play or not is of no consequence, as long as my team gets the job done.

Being double-teamed can be very dangerous. Sometimes you think you only have one blocker. And just when you believe you have him beaten, here comes another guy to help him out. At this point you really have to be cautious, because three different sets of legs and arms are all going in separate directions. The moment when you are on your way down to the turf is particularly dangerous, since most leg and knee injuries take place in that moment.

And then there's triple-teaming. Just when you have worked twice as hard fighting through two three-hundred-pound-plus "hogs" to see your way clear to the quarterback—bam, here comes a pesky running back to pick up where the linemen left off. He's fast, so you really have to watch out for him.

How Do You Combat Getting Hurt?

A football player must use the tools at his disposal to avoid injury. He can't let down his guard in the heat of battle and forget what's important.

One of the most vital assets a football player has is peripheral vision. When you are looking straight ahead at the ball carrier, you can still see out of the corner of your eyes what is approaching you on either side. This skill must be used at all times.

You always must be aware of your surroundings. If I'm rushing the passer and see a wide open lane to the ball car-

---

"One of the most vital assets a football player has is peripheral vision."

---

rier, I'm going for him. However, at the same time I have to be looking for a running back who will be trying to blindside me.

You always should know where your teammates are. We've practiced and played together long enough that we know where each of us will usually be in any given defensive alignment and movement.

And of course, you always know your opponent. I've mentioned how much time and how many days we spend watching and analyzing film of our opponents. There is just no substitute for properly preparing for a game and studying film of our adversaries. Game film tells us the offensive alignments where they might run a double-team or a crackback block. Sometimes we notice a certain stance the linemen take that might give away what the next play could be. You must study the film, or you will be lost at game time.

Another means of fighting off injuries and standing firm in the trenches is found in weight-lifting and conditioning by running. Building and strengthening the major muscles and joints of your body protects you from being hurt. I follow a rigid regimen in the weight room.

In the same way, running sprints and jogging helps to build stamina. Many injuries happen to athletes when they are tired and out of shape, since they are not as alert to protect themselves from being blindsided or victimized by a crackback block.

Training and conditioning must occur daily, especially during the off-season. The older I get, the more important training and conditioning become. Each day I miss my training and conditioning is a day that can never be made up. It's gone and somewhere, sometime, I will have to pay for it. I think the word here is discipline.

Finally, after I know my opponent, and have trained and conditioned my body, I must practice the right fundamentals.

Notice that I say the "right" fundamentals.

An old proverb says, "Practice makes perfect." That statement is only true if you are practicing what is right. Practicing the wrong fundamentals will never help, but rather will always hinder you. I have to practice my moves and techinque every time I hit the field. And when I think I know exactly what to do, I do it again.

When the game starts, it's too late to think about whether you're prepared or not. Your preparation will glaringly be displayed, good or bad, throughout the course of the game.

Problems on the Field of Life

You know, as a Christian, I run into the very same problems on a spiritual level that I do on the football field. I can get blindsided by friends or other people that don't understand me and what I stand for. I probably trust too many persons and when I'm not looking, I have received a crack-

---

"I've also been attacked for my beliefs by a double-team and a triple-team. How do I handle these threats to my faith? The same way I do as a football player."

---

back block mentally and sometimes physically. I've also been attacked for my beliefs by a double-team and a triple-team.

How do I handle these threats to my faith? The same way I do as a football player.

The first step is training. I must study God's Word on a daily basis. Paul wrote to Timothy:

> Be diligent [study] to present yourself approved to God as a workman who does not need to be ashamed, handling accurately the word of truth. (2 Timothy 2:15, NAS)

There is no way I will ever be able to deal with all that life has to offer without daily and diligently delving into God's Word. It's like watching game film. Trust is another factor. We also must be able to trust in Him. We are told to "Trust in the LORD with all your heart and lean not on your own understanding; in all your ways acknowledge him, and he will make your paths straight" (Proverbs 3:5–6).

The second focus is on my surroundings. I must also be careful not to surround myself too closely with those who don't believe in God's Word. I have many friends who are not Christians and I sure do love them. But we have a different relationship. Unbelievers just don't have as much in common as believers do. They don't have the same goals, morals, or social life that believers in Christ have.

It doesn't take too much sense to realize that you become like those with whom you spend the most time. Know your surroundings and control them; don't let your surroundings control you.

Finally, practice what you know is right. Too often we focus on doing what we've always done. We don't progress, keep in shape, work out daily. The warning is clear:

> In fact, though by this time you ought to be teachers, you need someone to teach you the elementary truths of God's word all over again. You need milk, not solid food! Anyone who lives on milk, being still an infant, is not acquainted with the teaching about righteousness. But solid food is for the mature, who by constant use have trained themselves to distinguish good from evil. (Hebrews 5:12–14)

I really like the way the Living Bible paraphrases verse 14:

> You will never be able to eat solid spiritual food and understand the deeper things of God's Word until you become better Christians and learn right from wrong by practicing doing right.

Man, that verse really says it all, doesn't it? Can you imagine a professional football player telling his coach, "Hey, this season I don't feel like lifting weights, running sprints, or attending any practices, and furthermore, I'm going to spend my time hanging around with the baseball team." What do you think his coach would tell him?

In the same way we as Christians must study God's Word, surround ourselves with other believers, and practice what is right. A football player knows if he doesn't show his commitment by his actions that he's off the team, his dream at an end. Christians need to know it also.

WHO KEEPS YOU ACCOUNTABLE?

Accountability seems to be a forgotten art these days in America. Everybody wants to do his own thing, and nobody wants to answer to anyone else except himself.

Can you imagine what a football team would be like if no one was accountable to someone else? The coach sends a play in during a game, and the quarterback doesn't like it so he changes it. The running backs don't want to follow the quarterback's call, so they decide to just stand still and watch, rather than run the ball. The receivers don't like either the quarterback's call or the running backs' decision; they want to go get some Gatorade on the sidelines. And on and on they would go, as the entire team would take matters into their own hands.

Where there is no accountability, there is chaos. Somebody must be in control.

The very same principle applies to a person's spiritual life. You cannot be in control of your own spirituality. You must be accountable to someone greater than yourself, someone who can call the shots on a daily basis.

Those of us who consider ourselves Christians have chosen Jesus Christ to be the coach of our lives. We believe that His Word, the Bible, contains everything we need to live the most abundant life possible on this earth. He promised this to us, if we would follow Him.

Therefore, Christians are accountable to Jesus Christ and His commands. We believe His guideline for our lives is best:

This is how we know that we love the children of God: by loving God and carrying out his commands. This is love for God: to obey his commands. And his commands are not burdensome. (1 John 5:2–3)

On a football team players are first accountable to the coach. Since the coach can't be on the field during the game, he appoints key players on the field to make sure his plans get carried out. On offense it's usually the quarterback that gives the instructions from the coach. On defense one of the linebackers gives the assignment on each play. Players know that during the game they must give the coach's designated captain the same attention they would give the coach.

And accountability doesn't stop with the quarterback and linebackers. Each player is responsible to his teammates for making the play successful; if he anticipates something happening, he should alert others of what he has observed.

For example, Byron Evans, one of the Eagles' linebackers, may notice the opposing team's alignment signifies the play is probably going to the left. He could then move up to the line of scrimmage and move Jerome Brown or Calvin Simmons one way or the other in order to stop the offense from gaining valuable yardage. In that situation, as a player I'm accountable to Byron, and Byron is accountable to the coach.

How This Works for Christians

Now what does all that mean to a Christian? Well, yes, we are accountable to God, but we must also be accountable to other Christians who are more mature in their faith.

After the Lord, I'm first of all accountable to my wife, Sara. I know I can depend on her to tell it like it is. God always uses Sara to affirm or negate whatever may surface in my life. Spiritually, I'm also accountable to some Christian friends who give me sound spiritual guidance. Jerry

Upton, Calvin Clark, R.V. Brown, Terry Minor, Art Moore, Joe Ward, Brett Fuller, and Lee Jenkins are all men to whom I can reveal my deepest thoughts and plans. I know they will shoot straight with me from their own experiences, as well as from God's Word.

Any one of them can talk to me for just a few minutes and discern whether I'm walking close to the Lord or if I might just need a spiritual kick in the seat of my pants. I can really count on them to tell me when I'm straying off the path—whether I ask to do so or not.

Who holds you accountable? You need someone to whom you can pour out your deepest thoughts and heartaches.

Let's look at what happens to many Christians when they choose not to be accountable to another Christian.

We all have blind spots, areas in our lives which hinder our spiritual growth, but areas we cannot see. For example,

---

"Who holds you accountable? You need someone to whom you can pour out your deepest thoughts and heartaches. . . . We all have blind spots, areas in our lives which hinder our spiritual growth, but areas we cannot see."

---

we may express anger to others in a manner that is actually verbally abusive. We feel justified in our correction of them, but another believer can help understand that our words should be the kind to inspire a positive response. In other words, there is a better way to express our anger, and we may need help finding that way.

If we are not accountable to someone else, we may never understand why people reject our advice. We must learn to accept constructive criticism ourselves. We set ourselves up for the problems in our lives that way. We have to understand the truth of the proverb: "Stern discipline awaits him who leaves the path; he who hates correction will die" (Proverbs 15:10). When we are accountable to another Christian, they can correct us when we mess up.

Some Christians say that they don't feel right pointing out other Christians' errors. That's true. We shouldn't be going around telling others their shortcomings, unless they ask you to. The only exception to this is if another Christian sins against you. The Lord directed us how to respond in this instance:

> If your brother sins against you, go and show him his fault, just between the two of you. If he listens to you, you have won your brother over. But if he will not listen, take one or two others along, so that "every matter may be established by the testimony of two or three witnesses." If he refuses to listen to them, tell it to the church; and if he refuses to listen even to the church, treat him as you would a pagan or a tax collector. (Matthew 18:15–17)

You see, when we are unaccountable, we have a tendency to gossip. A great definition of gossip is this: expressing your opinion about a matter when you are neither a part of the problem nor the solution.

The Necessity for Accountability

On a football team when a player continues to gripe about mistakes and hurts the team, you must go to him and tell him about it. Notice I say go to him, not to the other teammates. If you don't go to him, you are hurting the team as much as he is.

"If we do not place ourselves in an accountable relationship with other believers, we are in danger of running out of bounds and not even being aware of our mistake."

The same holds true spiritually in the body of Christ. If we do not place ourselves in an accountable relationship with other believers, we are in danger of running out of bounds and not even being aware of our mistake. There is just no telling how many sins committed by Christians could have been averted if some of these believers had been confronted by other Christians instead of criticized.

My pastor in Tennessee, Rev. Jerry Upton, had an incredible vision about the damage we do to ourselves. He says he was taken to a large hospital where he was given a tour conducted by the Lord. The hospital had three wards filled with many hurting Christians.

In the first ward about a hundred believers were discouraged and depressed because they had never gotten off the ground in their faith. The Lord told him not to worry about these people because they were cared for by several doctors and nurses, who were actually ministers and other mature believers who edified and built up the suffering Christians. These believers would be restored to good spiritual health because they were involved with other more mature Christians.

Then the Lord took my pastor to the second ward. Here people had been hurt more deeply than those in the first ward. He was told that these Christians had gone forth in spiritual warfare against the enemy and had been injured;

they needed repair and nurturing back to sound spiritual health. Fewer doctors and nurses were around, but the Lord assured him that these also would return to spiritual whole-ness because of the care they would receive.

Before he entered the third ward, however, the Lord told him to prepare his heart for something he had never witnessed. Even so, he couldn't believe his eyes when he entered that third ward. Some people's heads were half blown off; arms were missing from some, legs from others. But the difference from the other two wards was blatantly visible: Not one doctor and not one nurse ministered to these believers. They just lay there, with no hope for recov-ery. When my pastor asked the Lord who in the world these people were, the Lord's answer cut him to the very quick of his soul.

The Lord told him, "These believers have been wounded by other believers. There are no doctors or nurses because the first thing a Christian wounded by another Christian does is isolate himself from any form of ministry. Many of these probably won't make it back to spiritual wholeness."

The Bible tells us that Satan cannot touch a Christian un-less God gives him permission, as He did in the case of Job. So, how in the world can Satan get to believers? He accomplishes this by attacking Christians through other Christians. The only way a believer can be devoured by Satan is through another believer! Remember Paul's warn-ing: "If you keep on biting and devouring each other, watch out or you will be destroyed by each other" (Galatians 5:15).

Believers in Jesus Christ are accountable to each other. We must stop criticizing and seek to build each other up instead. And, yes, we must confront one another when nec-essary and practice accountability at all costs. We must do as the Apostle John reminds us: "All men will know that you are my disciples, if you love one another" (John 13:35).

The old song goes, "And they will know we are Christians by our love." We have got to start getting along with other Christians, regardless of what label they wear. We

---

"So, how in the world can Satan get to believers? He accomplishes this by attacking Christians through other Christians."

---

must stop running down other churches and believers just because their relationship with the Lord is not like ours.

The common ground for fellowship with other Christians is their belief in and following of Jesus Christ. Not doctrine, not form of worship, not dress, not hair style—a simple belief in and acceptance of Jesus Christ as Lord and Savior is all that is required.

Even the disciples struggled with this:

> "Master," said John, "we saw a man driving out demons in your name and we tried to stop him, because he is not one of us."
>
> "Do not stop him," Jesus said, "for whoever is not against you is for you." (Luke 9:49)

John was upset because the guy was not a part of their group. We do not have the right to tell someone what they are doing is not of God unless we know it contradicts Scripture—and then we'd better know exactly what Scripture we're talking about.

John was accountable to Jesus, and Jesus kept him accountable. Who will keep you accountable so you will not become another Christian casualty? Who will hold you to the shining example God has called you to be?

Until we as the body of Christ get right with each other, we're never going to solve the abortion problem. We're never going to have any effect on the divorce rate among Christians. As a matter of fact, we're never going to accomplish anything, until we learn to love each other as God commands us to do.

As followers of Jesus Christ, we have to get serious about *practicing* accountability or the world will continue to call Christianity just another religion. The proof must be in the way we live our lives.

SAY IT WHETHER YOU FEEL LIKE IT OR NOT!

I really believe in evangelism. *Webster's New Collegiate Dictionary* defines *evangelism* as "the winning of personal commitments to Christ." I like that; even a secular dictionary has an excellent definition.

Evangelism is so much a part of my natural state of being that I often make statements evangelistically without even thinking. For example, we were playing the Washington Redskins and were just slightly behind when the first half ended.

I had played a tough thirty minutes of football and was running toward the tunnel that led to our assigned locker room. As I slowed down to a trot to enter the tunnel, I heard my name called by a fan up in the stands over my head.

Here we were the visiting team in Washington. Maybe an Eagles fan had come all the way to Washington, D.C., to see us play. Or maybe a fellow Christian brother just wanted to say hello and encourage me in my faith. Of course, I looked up.

"You Need Jesus!"

Well, I was wrong. Much to my dismay, I saw a young man holding up a T-shirt with an obscene message, using one of the most hideous four-letter words in the English language.

Most players just ignore ridiculous actions such as this from fans, but something inside me made me respond to this guy. I could have said many things. As a matter of fact, a part of me wanted to get my hands on him and maybe make him eat that shirt.

95

However, the first words that came out of my mouth were, "Hey, man, you need Jesus!"

Simple, but profound. I waited to see if he had a comeback. Silence and a look of embarrassment were all he could give.

Then a woman sitting near him who had witnessed the whole affair, shouted to the man, "You're right, Reggie. He does need Jesus!" At this the guy sat down and folded up his very distasteful shirt. After the half was over and we were running through the tunnel to return to the field, I made a special effort to look for that man with the T-shirt.

As I scanned the section of seats where he was sitting, I finally spotted him. The shirt was gone, out of sight.

Later that week following the game, we had our regular team Bible study after practice. A few of my Christian brothers on the Eagles—Harper LaBel, Bruce Collie, and Matt Darwin—gathered in a team meeting room beneath Veterans' Stadium.

On this day the topic was sharing our faith. One of the guys said he really appreciated what I had told the fan during halftime of the Redskins' game. The other guys didn't know what he was talking about, so he related the whole story to them.

When he had finished telling the story, one of my other teammates asked, "Isn't that being a little too bold? What if you turned the guy off by mentioning that he needs Jesus?" I was really caught off guard, not quite sure how to answer in my own defense. Why had I responded in the manner I did?

Then before I could get a single word out of my mouth, another teammate spoke up for me. He said, "Hey, that's Reggie. If it were you or me, it might have been wrong for us to say what he did. But that's the way Reggie White is every day."

He was right. That is the way I am. I didn't stop to think about what was the correct theological statement to expound at that precise moment. I just opened my mouth and the words "You need Jesus" came flying out.

Can We Be Too Bold?

To me that's what evangelism is all about. Just saying what you are led to say, and then leaving the results up to the Holy Spirit. The Scriptures tell us, "Whatever you do, work

---

"I didn't stop to think about what was the correct theological statement to expound at that precise moment. I just opened my mouth and the words 'You need Jesus' came flying out."

---

at it with all your heart, as working for the Lord, not for men" (Colossians 3:23).

We are walking witnesses for Jesus Christ everywhere we go. How can we do less than witness with all our heart. Our styles may be different, but the intensity shouldn't be. I know all Christians can't do it in the same manner as I do, but I have no choice but to do it with all my heart.

A. C. Green is a Christian brother who plays for the Los Angeles Lakers basketball team. He told me that a reporter once asked him how a Christian could play a game like NBA basketball, a game with so much physical contact. A. C.'s response was that his life on the basketball court is the same as his life off the hardwood. He's going to be aggressive and give it all he's got both on and off the court—on, to win the game for his team; off, to win people for Christ.

God has given me an incredible platform as an NFL professional football player. The reason I'm in Philadelphia today is that that's exactly where God wants me to serve Him right now. And any time I have a chance to proclaim Jesus Christ as Lord, I'm going to do it. Period!

I may not always be as popular or have as visible a platform as I do right now while I'm still playing football. I can't do less than I am right now.

One way I make use of my platform is in one of the many lower income neighborhoods in Philadelphia. Often on Friday afternoons during football season, my family and I and maybe a couple of the Eagles' football players travel to one of the local schoolyards.

Why take my family into such a hostile environment? You see, I want those precious people to see that some black families stay together and enjoy loving each other. And I want my family to understand that we have a responsibility to others as well.

On one particular Friday, tight end Keith Jackson and cornerback Eric Allen accompanied me to the playground. We drove my van, completely unannounced, onto the playground right smack dab next to the basketball court.

Keith and Eric helped me unload the huge black speakers from the back of the van, connecting all the wires from the speakers to the "boom box." Then it was time to find some electricity.

I took the one-hundred-foot extension cord and went door to door asking if we could plug into their outlet. As usual, I got a "yes" from the first family that was at home.

Trying to block a kick against my nemisis offensive line, the Redskins!

They retired my jersey at Howard High School in Chattanooga.

Charles Morgan and I during my Howard High days. He is a special player.

High school district basketball champs!

I still can't believe I used to jump that high. I guess it's easier at 230 lbs. than at 285 lbs.

My family and I after the UT Orange/White game in my sophomore year. Sister: Christie Collier, cousin: Christopher Tillison, mother:Thelma Collier, step-father:Leonard Collier.

Bob Hope and I during the television show with the Kodak All-Americans!

I really enjoyed this conversation with coach Bear Byrant, especially since we had just finished beating his football team!

Jackie Davidson has always been an enthusiastic part of my life.

I really did enjoy playing with the USFL Memphis Showboats.

The beginning of my married life with my best friend, Sara.

Jeremy Reginald, our first born.

Our Christmas picture (1989).

Jeremy thinks the photographer disappeared in the flash! (Christmas 1988).

Jecolia Regara, our daughter.

Jecolia Regara, 3 years old.

Jeremy Reginald, 5 years old.

My father,
Charles White.

My mother, Thelma Collier,
and my sister, Christie.

Herman Prater and I shared a lot of love
during my Jr. High years. He is still a
great friend and the best photographer.

Sara with her best friend of 25 years, Valerie. Boy, what great inspiration.

"Hope Palace" for young, homeless, pregnant women.

Sara and her parents, Charles and Maria Copeland.

Buddy Ryan could say anything about me. He's the Boss.

Getting "my turn" at a roast held in my honor!

March 1987

Sara, Jeremy and I are ending the roast with great memories. Sara had a lot to say, too.

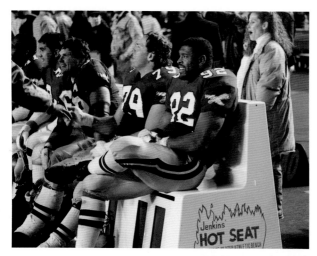

You wouldn't believe how hot that seat gets during some games!

This is the quarterback's view of me running 70 yards for my first NFL touchdown.

Photo/Richard B. Gentile

I'm trying to explain to the offensive line that there is no need to curse at an opposing player just because they fail to carry out their assignment!

Photo/Ed Mahan

This is definitely going to hurt you, Joe, more than it is me.

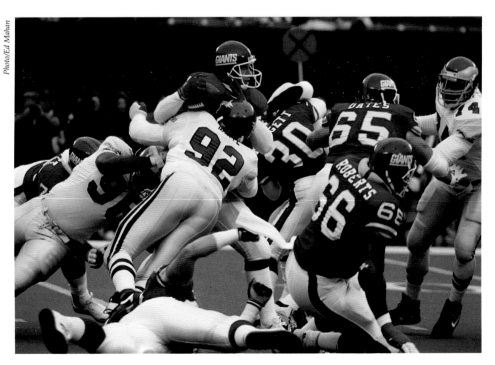

Photo/Ed Mahan

Goodbye Mr. Simms.

Hello, Mr. Marino.

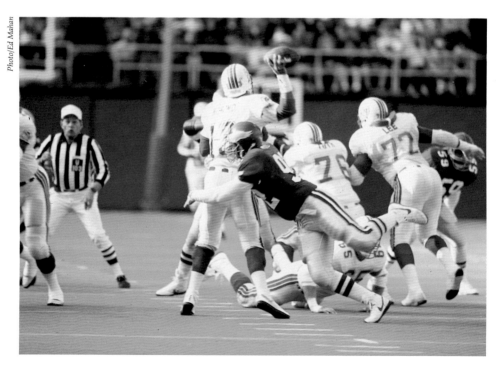

In the grasp? I think so.

Do you see holding? I see holding.

You've got to be kidding.

Here we are in 1991! God is Great!

The North Philadelphia Playgrounds

The situation is the same as always, and this playground is much like others you have seen either firsthand or in movies and other videos about the inner city. Its colors are drab and dull and downright depressing. There are no trees and certainly never any grass—just good old black asphalt, hard and hot and dirty.

> *"God has given me an incredible platform as an NFL professional football player. The reason I'm in Philadelphia today is that that's exactly where God wants me to serve Him right now."*

About ten to fifteen kids play on the basketball court. It doesn't take these kids long to come around to see who is getting out of the new van and setting up equipment.

Two or more guys well over six feet tall and weighing two hundred fifty plus, in decent physical condition, do draw some attention as maybe being professional athletes. The kids come. If we were not football players, we could probably pass for a couple of wrestlers.

We put on some Christian rap music and turn the speakers up to full tilt. You can literally hear the music for several blocks. Jeremy helps me rap a song or two.

My teammates and I then start autographing stacks of Philadelphia Eagles' team pictures for the kids. Young kids, teenagers, and adults alike gather around us to receive an autographed picture. On this particular day even a couple of policemen stopped by to see what was going on.

Sara and our children have a great time dancing with the other kids and trying to learn the latest techniques of group rope jumping. Sara still can't figure out how they perform the "Double Dutch" jump, but she is determined to perfect it on one of our future visits.

Within forty-five minutes to an hour, our crowd has grown to several hundred interested bystanders. They all have the same question, why would some highly paid professional football players take valuable time to be with them in their neighborhood? No promotional tour, no sponsored event.

After we have literally signed several hundred autographs, I grab the microphone and tell the crowd to please give me their attention. Everyone gets quiet as I tell them to please have a seat on the asphalt, because I want to tell them why we are here.

Always a few older teenagers continue playing basketball, and I have to invite them, sometimes forcefully, to bring their ball over to our group and listen to what I have to say. They stop their game and come over.

Usually I ask a very talented friend of mine and Sara's, Miki Kornegay, to sing a gospel song to settle everyone down. Then I take the mike and begin to explain why we are there.

I remind them that I grew up in a neighborhood just like theirs. I know what it's like to feel frustrated, to search for peace and a sense of security. I tell them about my upbringing and the most important thing I learned as a kid. I tell them about God and about His love for me.

I tell them that I love them with the love of the Lord Jesus Christ who loved them so much that He gave His life for them. I share that nothing in life satisfies like He does, that they may think power or money or important friends may fill the need they have. I read a few passages of Scripture and then relay to them the plan of salvation. As their heads are bowed on that dirty, old, hot playground, several of the kids pray to receive Christ as their Lord and Savior.

"I think alcohol has been the cause of problems for so many people, and I need to voice my opposition to it."

The rest of the crowd is dismisssed as I remind them that we will be back the next Friday and that they should tell their friends and bring them back with them. Then I take the kids who have prayed to receive Christ over to the side and explain to them further what has just happened to their lives as a result of asking Jesus to come into their hearts. The next week I talk with them again about the problems they have, about what being a Christian is all about. What a glorious time we have on those Fridays.

Why do I take time out of my hectic schedule to be with these kids in North Philadelphia? Because God has given me a platform, and if I don't use it, I commit sin. Therefore, I choose to obey my Lord. And I enjoy it.

Many athletes today are automatically associated with beer and alcoholic beverages. I want kids to know that not all athletes lend their names and faces to this industry. Some of us stand for Jesus Christ and make no apologies about avoiding beer and alcoholic beverages.

My personal conviction makes me refuse to have my picture in the Philadelphia Eagles' calendar, which features several of the players each month because it is sponsored by an alcoholic beverage company. I think alcohol has been the cause of problems for so many people, and I need to voice my opposition to it.

I'm against beer and alcohol and everything it stands for. I even have my name withdrawn each year from the lineman of the year competition, because it also is sponsored by an alcoholic beverage company. I want the name Reggie White associated with wholesome activities, ones that don't harm people's minds and bodies.

You know, we don't have to go knocking on doors to be a witness for Jesus Christ. All we have to do is get up every morning and live our lives to the fullest. Whether we want to be a witness or not, we are; what matters is the kind of witness we have.

When you have the opportunity, don't duck. Be bold, be natural and share only what is on your heart and mind. Then leave the results up to the Holy Spirit.

Boldness means just do it!

IF YOUR SPEECH ISN'T BUILDING SOMEONE UP, KEEP QUIET!

Handling criticism doesn't come easily for most of us. People say—and write—things about others that simply aren't true, judging their motives and actions and even character incorrectly. It's frustrating when you come up against that, but what's even more frustrating is when a so-called Christian is the one making the criticism.

That's probably the biggest problem we have in the church today—criticism. I believe that that's the only way Satan can hinder Christians—by working through other Christian believers. You know, the Bible teaches that God will not let Satan touch believers directly.

He doesn't have to. We can't keep our mouths shut when we have nothing good to say. I really believe that that's why the world laughs at Christianity. We just don't practice what the Bible says about edifying and building each other up.

In football, a player can have all the right playbooks, the best coaches, supportive teammates, and the finest equipment and sports facility available. But if he doesn't practice, practice, practice—he might as well quit because he'll be crushed by the reality of the game.

I really enjoyed a conference held at our church in Maryville and led by a minister named Rick Joyner.* The whole workshop was devoted to eliminating criticism among Christians—learning how to pray, rather than ac-

---

* I am indebted to Rick Joyner (*Morningstar Prophetic Journal,* P.O.Box 369, Pineville, N.C. 28134) for much of the material in this chapter.

cuse others. Sounds great in principle, but how do we put it into practice?

Who's Our Accuser?

The accuser of the Christians is called by many names, but let's just call a spade a spade and give him his biblical name, Satan. Satan accuses believers before God day and night (Revelation 12:10). It's probably his number one job. The more he has access to our lives by our lack of closeness in our walk with Christ, the more he can use us to accuse and criticize. And how does Satan actually confront and accuse followers of Jesus? He accomplishes this by using us against each other.

If the devil were to come walking down the aisle of your church on Sunday morning wearing a red suit with cape, long horns on his head, and a pitch fork, he would be immediately recognized. So Satan has to use the ultimate disguise—that of another Christian. Getting Christians to turn against other Christians is his specialty. Nothing pleases him more than to cause division, because he can't work when the church is unified. Well, by looking at the divisions between denominations and churches today, I would say he is having a good time.

He knows that authority that has been given to every believer, but most *believers* don't. And as a result Satan is winning this battle hands down. And we are letting him do it without even realizing what is happening.

"Territorial Preservation"

Reverend Joyner calls "territorial preservation" the main culprit in keeping Christians divided. This occurs when a Christian takes his own opinion too seriously, making it his

> **"Satan has to use the ultimate disguise—that of another Christian. Getting Christians to turn against other Christians is his specialty. Nothing pleases him more than to cause division, because he can't work when the church is unified."**

gospel. When that happens, our true spiritual authority is powerless, and we are even more susceptible to becoming an accuser.

Sometimes a football player can start thinking he's the only one who knows what to do. He'll start offering his opinion during films and team meetings. He'll get so worked up trying to prove to his teammates how great he is that he'll find himself all alone. The more he accuses others of slacking off, the more his own performance suffers.

Jesus told His disciples, "For whoever wants to save his life will lose it, but whoever loses his life for me will find it" (Matthew 16:25).

Try as we might, there is no way to turn this principle around. Never will you gain anything spiritually by inverting the above.

The prophet Isaiah explained the same thing in different words:

Then your light will break forth like the dawn, and your healing will quickly appear; then your righteousness will go before you, and the glory of the LORD will be your rear guard. Then you will call, and the LORD will answer; you will cry for help, and he will say: Here am I. "If you do away with the yoke of oppression, with the pointing finger and malicious talk, and if you spend yourselves on behalf of the hungry and satisfy the needs of the oppressed, then your light will rise in the darkness, and your night will become like the noonday." (Isaiah 58:8–10)

Our Own Worst Enemies

Maybe you feel as if you have no power in your spiritual life. Do you wonder if the Lord is even listening to you when you pray? Instead of walking in the Spirit, you question where the spirit is. It could be that you have the sin of the "pointing finger and malicious talk."

What is this pointing finger? Well, I think it is those times when we are unable to accept the responsibility of our own sin and attempt to transfer it to someone else. It happens all the time on the football field.

I may get beat on a play and not be able to put any pressure on the quarterback whatsoever. The easy thing for me to say is, "Hey, I got double-teamed. So there is no way I'm responsible for that touchdown pass being completed. You guys (pointing my finger at the other defensive linemen) should have put more pressure on him."

Instead, I have to admit that I always get double-teamed and have to constantly learn more and better techniques to get through them to the passer. My job in passing situations is to put pressure on the quarterback, even if I'm quadruple-teamed. Pointing the finger toward others only makes matters worse, for me as well as the others.

What does malicious talk mean? The dictionary describes maliciousness as a desire to harm others or see others suffer.

How in the world could any Christian be malicious? It's easy! Most Christians commit this sin on a daily basis. We do this outwardly in our speech and most certainly inwardly in our thoughts. And then there are those times when we act maliciously without even being conscious of our actions. Then when we are confronted about our sin, we just shrug it off and refuse to deal with it. Boy, does Satan have a blast when we refuse to confess and repent of known sin. We can read what happens next in the book of Proverbs: "But the way of the wicked is like deep darkness; they do not know what makes them stumble" (4:19).

I don't believe that verse is just speaking to unbelievers, but also to Christians. When we are out of fellowship with

---

"When we are confronted about our sin, we just shrug it off and refuse to deal with it. Boy, does Satan have a blast when we refuse to confess and repent of known sin."

God, we stumble in the darkness until we renew our relationship with Him. And how do we get right with God?

> But if we walk in the light, as he is in the light, we have fellowship with one another, and the blood of Jesus, his Son, purifies us from every sin. (1 John 1:7)

The more light we walk in, the more our light increases. And the more the light increases, the more darkness that is exposed.

Isn't it also amazing that the critical person is usually not very critical of himself? Jesus confronted His disciples on that very issue:

> Why do you look at the speck of sawdust in your brother's eye and pay no attention to the plank in your

own eye? How can you say to your brother, "Let me take the speck out of your eye," when all the time there is a plank in your own eye? You hypocrite, first take the plank out of your own eye, and then you will see clearly to remove the speck from your brother's eye. (Matthew 7:3–5)

Simply stated, when you have confessed and repented of your own sins, then and only then can you approach your brother about his sin. Do we do this? Of course not! Instead, we maliciously talk and point our finger when we should be interceding in prayer and speaking with our brother in private.

Don't you realize that when you criticize another brother or sister, you are being critical of a creation of our God. And we are actually telling God that His workmanship doesn't meet up to our standards. And can anybody really change somebody else?

When we find fault with someone's children, who will be offended? Of course, their parents would be. Well, why wouldn't God feel the same way when we criticize His children? When we judge one of His creatures, aren't we in essence judging God Himself? Could the same be said when we judge one of His leaders? Could we not be judging His leadership?

The Epistles teach us this very lesson. James wrote:

Brothers, do not slander one another. Anyone who speaks against his brother or judges him, speaks against the law and judges it. When you judge the law, you are not keeping it, but sitting in judgment on it. There is only one Lawgiver and Judge, the one who is able to save and destroy. But you—who are you to judge your neighbor? (James 4:11–12)

When we start judging others, we yoke ourselves. That's right, we yoke or bind ourselves from the blessings that come from being in right relationship with Jesus Christ. I

"Isn't it also amazing that the critical person is usually not very critical of himself?"

know this: I don't want to be bound by anything, especially by my own doing.

Pride is another sin that can cause us to have a critical spirit. And the Bible tells us that pride brings what no Christian would ever want to have—God's opposition. Just as humility brings blessing: "But he gives us more grace. That is why Scripture says: 'God opposes the proud but gives grace to the humble'" (James 4:6).

Man, I don't ever want God to be in opposition to me. But that is exactly what James tells us God is, when we have pride in our lives.

Our criticism must be grounded in real discernment. For example, our brother may be living in open sin and needs to be confronted. We are told (Matthew 18) precisely how to confront our brother and restore him to wholeness in Christ. We are also told what to do if he refuses to repent of his sin.

Many excuses are given for not enforcing the Matthew 18 principle in churches today. One of the most often mentioned excuses is "They probably won't listen to me." Whatever the excuse may be, we are commanded not to accuse our brothers, but rather to intercede for them, be the go-between to restore them to the body of Christ.

We are not supposed to use Matthew 18 as a stick to beat our brother because he has offended us, either. We must do all things in love and never in defending our pride or in retaliation.

Our Model of Correction

Our model in correction must be the Lord Jesus Christ Himself. He gives a perfect example in His correction of the seven churches in the book of Revelation.

He began by first of all praising each church and pointing out what they were doing right. Then He directly identified their problems. After this He gave each church an incredible promise of a reward for overcoming their obstacles.

Even today, God never changes. When He corrects us, He always gives those who overcome great promises and encouragement.

Jesus always encourages and gives hope; Satan always comdemns and seeks to discourage believers. Jesus constantly edifies and imparts confidence in overcoming problems; Satan loves to humiliate and shame you into quitting. Jesus loves us and wants to take us to sit next to Him at His Father's side; Satan clearly wants to destroy us.

Let's look at what God promises when we don't point the finger and practice malicious talk.

> Then your light will rise in the darkness, and your night will become like the noonday. The LORD will guide you always: he will satisfy your needs in a sun-scorched land and will strengthen your frame. You will be like a well-watered garden, like a spring whose waters never fail. (Isaiah 58:10–11)

Wow! What a promise! What else could any Christian ask for?

There can only be two forms of power in this world, God's and Satan's. When we carry out things in our own power and not by the authority of the Holy Spirit, are we not applying the power of Satan, and perhaps even practicing a form of Satanism? Which power are you using in your criticism?

> *"Jesus always encourages and gives hope; Satan always comdemns and seeks to discourage believers. Jesus constantly edifies and imparts confidence in overcoming problems; Satan loves to humiliate and shame you into quitting."*

Hey, I don't want to preach at you or try to tell you how I have this problem under control. I don't. The point of the finger and malicious talk is something I will have to work on the rest of my life. But I am recognizing that this problem is something every Christian must address.

Let's really put all our energies into avoiding accusations and instead, turn them into intercession on behalf of our Christian brothers and sisters. Let's be aware of our habits of speech. If we aren't building others up by our words, then maybe we'd best keep quiet indeed.

PART ✦ THREE

FAMILY

BLACK
FAMILY MINISTRY

Examine these statistics: They reflect a sad reality and an immediate need.

- 25 percent of all abortions in this country are performed on black women (489,000 in 1989).

- 14 percent of the future black race has been eliminated since 1973 (source: Black Americans for Life).

- 2 out of every 3 youths locked up in state-run institutions are either black, Hispanic, or members of another ethnic or racial minority.

- 1 out of every 4 black men between 20 and 29 years of age is either in prison, on probation, or on parole from prison.

- A black man has a 1 in 21 chance of being murdered before he is 25 years old.

- The leading cause of death among black men 15 to 24 years of age is murder.

- 34 percent of the adult population in prison in the United States is black (*Ebony Magazine* and the *Children in Custody Census*).

Incredibly alarming statistics, whether you are black or white, but especially if you are black.

Isn't what is happening among the black neighborhoods true in most communities? No. For example, in the city of Memphis, Tennessee, 99 percent of the murders committed in a single year were committed black on black. And these numbers in Memphis are by no means abnormal compared to other cities across our nation. The number one cause of death in white communities is not murder, but it is in black communities! Black communities are in real trouble, to say the least.

The above facts are part of the reason that I believe God has led me into a ministry among blacks and the inner city. He has called me there to be His servant.

Some may say, "Wait a minute, Reggie, aren't you being racist with your Christianity?"

No way. Since I began sharing the gospel when I was a student at the University of Tennessee, more than 80 percent of my audiences have been Caucasian. And more than 60 percent of the souls that have been won to Christ under my ministry have been white. I know souls don't have any color, but I also know that the number of persons sharing the gospel among white people compared to those among black people is way out of proportion.

Yes, I know that the gospel is spoken to all people. However, the average black person, for whatever reason, will not as easily receive the gospel from a white minister.

When I first heard these statistics I cited, I was shocked beyond all comprehension. I promised God right then and there that I would strive with every part of my being to be the positive black Christian role model He commands me to be. And when my athletic career is over, I will use what platform I have left to minister to the people of the inner city. Sara and I both have made this promise to the Lord.

How Did This Happen?

How in the world did black families and inner city families get into such bad shape? One of the reasons is that these families have very few, if any, godly role models. How many evangelical black ministers or black Christian leaders can you name or even recognize? Another problem prevalent among black and inner city neighborhoods is that the people will not come to hear the gospel; you have to take it to them. That's why my family and I go to the North Philly

---

"I know souls don't have any color, but I also know that the number of persons sharing the gospel among white people compared to those among black people is way out of proportion."

---

neighborhoods weekly during the football season and to the inner city in Knoxville, Tennessee, during the off-season.

It's very sad, but very true, that a white brother cannot go into a black community and have a totally effective ministry with black people. Blacks in the inner city still do not trust white people and still blame them for the living conditions tolerated today. It is going to take some committed Christian black brothers and sisters—along with the help of some white Christians—to see an improvement in the way people actually live.

I'll never forget my pastor, Jerry Upton, sharing a conversation he had with a young black boy. He asked the young man what he wanted to be when he grew up.

The little boy responded, "I want to be 'the man.'"

"The man?" Jerry asked.

"Yeah, 'the man.' You know, the man who sells the stuff, the runner," he explained.

You see, "the man" has it all and doesn't have to work hard. He doesn't have to go to school. He doesn't have to get a job and work. He wears designer clothes and drives a new Mercedes or Cadillac and always has beautiful women hanging all over him. And he's usually not a drug addict.

Just think. Keep yourself clean as a kid and you can become a drug pusher and make life a total hell for all of your friends and neighbors. It doesn't make much sense, does it? But it certainly does if you're a black kid living in the inner city. Then it seems the easiest way out.

Another problem black families in the inner city experience is the absence of men in most of the families. Most black kids grow up in single parent homes, since many black men father children and then leave.

I think it is sad that these black men have used women as tools for their own enjoyment instead of seeing women as vessels God created to be respected and loved. Women should be treated as equals and companions and not something men use and then throw away when they're finished.

People wonder why women are the center of almost all black families. It's because there is no father in the home to be the leader. Why do you think all those professional athletes on national television always say hi to their moms?

Moms are in control in most black families and when a daughter grows up and marries, she knows no other way, but to be in control of the family just like her mother was. And black men, having been raised by mothers alone, have no idea what a real father should be.

When it comes to spending money in "missions," many churches care much more about the lost people in Africa and China than they do about the kids they pass on the way to work every day. We pray for God to stop the flow and intake of drugs, but few are willing to step in physically and intervene in the name of Christ. We've just gotten too comfortable in our suburban lives to worry about the inner cities. We've forgotten our mandate:

"For I was hungry and you gave me nothing to eat, I was thirsty and you gave me nothing to drink, I was a stranger and you did not invite me in, I needed clothes and you did not clothe me, I was sick and in prison and you did not look after me." They also will answer, "Lord, when did we see you hungry or thirsty or a stranger or needing clothes or sick or in prison, and did not help you?" He will reply, "I tell you the truth, whatever you did not do for one of the least of these, you did not do for me." (Matthew 25:42–45)

"Another problem black families in the inner city experience is the absence of men in most of the families. Most black kids grow up in single parent homes, since many black men father children and then leave."

Ministry to the Inner City

Are you or your church guilty of not having any ministry, financial or personal, to the inner city? Many Christians are scared to even drive through "that part of town" and definitely have no intentions of taking part in a ministry there. And yet, considering Jesus' words, do we really have a choice in the matter?

How do churches minister in the inner city? They just can't go into the streets, lead people through the four spiritual laws, pray for them, and then leave. That's what has been happening in the past, and it doesn't work.

Many valid inner city ministries need help from fellow Christian churches, and not just financially. People in the inner city need to see black and white Christians working together under black leadership to help them meet their needs where they are. Then after they see some needs being met, they will consider the Jesus the black and white Christians serve.

Rosie Grier, a former football player and dear friend, told me that he recently led a young man in the inner city to the Lord. After he had finished praying, the new Christian asked Rosie if he would help him find a job. Finding or helping to create new jobs would be an incredible ministry for a church.

All Talk and No Walk

Scores of people want to have their lives changed, but they see very few churches who attempt to minister to their needs. Many churches just are not willing to practice this:

> They overcame him by the blood of the Lamb and by the word of their testimony; they did not love their lives so much as to shrink from death. (Revelation 12:11)

When churches start caring less about their own needs and more about the needs of others, then we'll be ready to carry out the Great Commission. Right now many of us are so busy worrying about church doctrine and the superiority of one church over another church that we don't even have the same goal.

We have to work as one. The New York Giants didn't win the Super Bowl by having different goals. They all had the one same goal, with each player having a different part in order to accomplish the ultimate goal.

One hundred and twenty Christians were in the Upper Room on the day of Pentecost. They left that place of "one accord" and won more than three thousand people to the Lord.

In the same way, our churches must show a united front to the world so they might see that we have the answer for them. The Bible says that the world will know that we are Christians by our "love for one another."

We must first show that we can get along with one another. We are a family. Sure, we disagree and have fights, but we also work to find a solution and return to the "common bond" we have in Jesus Christ which is our true basis for fellowship.

Denominations must stop their feelings of superiority over others. We are on the same team with the same goal:

> If you have any encouragement from being united with Christ, if any comfort from his love, if any fellowship with the Spirit, if any tenderness and compassion, then make my joy complete by being like-minded, having the same love, being one in spirit and purpose. Do nothing out of selfish ambition or vain conceit, but in humility consider others better than yourselves. Each of you should look not only to your own interests, but also to the interests of others. (Philippians 2:1–4)

Being Diligent Where We Are Called

My family and I are members of a racially mixed church in Maryville, Tennessee, a beautiful little town outside of Knoxville. Our church members, black and white, believe in ministering to the inner city of Knoxville, to present Jesus Christ and to provide positive role models for the people who live there.

Our church opens a recreation center in the projects every day after school and on Saturdays. Good positive Christian role models from our church like Terry Minor and James Davis spend time with these kids, sharing with them and becoming a part of their everyday lives.

When that recreation center opened, we used the opportunity to state our goal for the center. Our speaker system blasted out Christian music that could be heard several blocks away. When music wasn't playing, we broadcast our bold stand for Jesus Christ and that together we were going to run all the drug pushers out of those projects. We told the pushers that they might as well get ready, because they were going to do battle with Jesus.

I grew up in the projects and came from a single parent home. Yes, I now live in a big house and drive an expensive car. But I know that inside my heart I'm the same person now that I was when I was living in the projects in Chattanooga. I also know that if God called me to give up that big house and that nice car or anything else that I have, so be it. It's His anyway.

I do have more treasure here on earth than most people, but I know where my true treasure lies. My treasure is in what I give away in obedience to the Lord, not in what I accumulate.

You may say, "What difference can one person really make? You can't win every black neighborhood in America to Jesus Christ." That may be true. But as I heard someone else say, "Just because you are not the complete answer to a problem doesn't mean you should fail to do what you *are* responsible for."

This reminds me of one of my most exciting moments in professional football. We were playing the Redskins in Washington, D.C., in a crucial Eastern divisional game in 1987. The opening game of the season against our archrivals would probably set the tone for all our matchups for the rest of the season. We were trailing in the game and our offense needed a lift in the worse sort of way.

Now, the Redskins have the best offensive line I play against almost every year, and this year was no exception. I had spent just about the whole game being double- and triple-teamed and was frustrated. It's hard to experience the

---

"My treasure is in what I give away in obedience to the Lord, not in what I accumulate."

---

ultimate satisfaction of a defensive player—which is sacking the quarterback—when you are consistently fighting off two and three "hogs" (an affectionate name for the Redskins' offensive line) all the time.

But I couldn't give up. I was going to get to their quarterback, Doug Williams, sooner or later. And I hoped it would be sooner.

We lined up on an obvious passing down situation, and I prepared to take on two blockers again and rush the quarterback. I slowly but surely pushed them back toward the pocket, when all of a sudden they both hit the ground and left me standing.

As I looked around for the quarterback, I noticed he still hadn't thrown the ball. I reached for him with both hands, and to my amazement, one of my hands fell directly on top of the football. I believe that Doug Williams was so shocked to see me, he forgot to hold onto the ball.

I too was a bit surprised to be so close to him and the ball. So I grabbed him with one hand, and all in one motion

I jerked the ball out of his clutch with my other hand and instinctively started to run with the ball.

As I looked up toward the goal line, I couldn't believe how far it was. You see, defensive lineman don't get to become running backs very often. It looked as if a touchdown was at least a good mile away; to a two-hundred-and-eighty-five-pound lineman those seventy yards might as well have been two miles.

I ran and I ran and I kept on running until finally I stumbled across the goal line and then was crushed by my own teammates. I had scored my first NFL touchdown and more importantly at the very time when my team really needed an emotional lift. And what a lift we got! For the first time, we were finally ahead on the scoreboard.

I had been given credit for a sack, forcing a fumble, recovering a fumble, and scoring a touchdown all on the same play. Wow, I had accomplished on one play what most guys would dream of doing in an entire game.

When the gun sounded ending the ballgame, the score was 34–24. What an incredible game, except for the fact that the Redskins had the 34. The most exciting moment in my football career, and we lost the game.

What's Your Measure of Success?

As I look back on that game, it would have been easy to feel like my efforts were all for nothing, because we lost.

After all, I had poured every ounce of energy into that game—and all for a loss?

Wrong!

My diligence in my time on the field and in practice for that Redskins game will pay off later in another game. The litmus test of my efforts during a game is not determined by the scoreboard, but inside my heart where I don't compare my play against another person's play. I look at how well I played compared to how well I could have played.

In the same way, I know I can't reach every person in the world with the gospel of Jesus Christ. I won't even come close to reaching all the black families in America even if I spend the rest of my life trying. But knowing that I may not be the total answer will not stop me from doing what I have been called to do.

I am the answer for the areas God has called me to right now. And those areas are the neighborhoods in North Philly and the project community in Knoxville.

I'm not just dreaming; I'm doing something about it! If I am going to be obedient to the Lord, I have no choice.

What're your North Philly and Knoxville projects? Are they at work, at school, or at home? Some valid evangelical ministries beg for volunteer help from committed Christians.

Remember, if you are not part of the solution, you are a definite part of the problem!

A serious congregation can take many avenues in fulfilling the great commission in the inner city. Dr. E. V. Hill, a great black pastor in the Watts area of Los Angeles, California, developed what is called the Step Program. It's a fantastic way for suburban white churches to get involved with an inner city ministry.

You know, finding a way to minister is not the problem. An old proverb says, "When the student is ready to learn, a teacher will appear." What an incredible truth.

When churches are ready, the ways and means of ministry to the inner city will always be there, crying out for us to complete our Christian responsibility.

Think about it. Pray about it. And then, do something.

SARA: THE REALITY OF A GODLY WOMAN

I love to tell this story. While I was at the University of Tennessee, I dated three girls, but I couldn't decide which one God wanted me to marry. I was diligently seeking God's will in preparation for marriage. I prayed really hard asking God to reveal who would be my wife. That night I had a dream that Sara and I were attending church. I woke up with such a peace concerning my marital destiny. A few years later after our foundation was formed, Sara and I were married.

As my wife, Sara proves to me more and more everyday just how much God loves me. If I could have written down what I wanted in a wife, she is all of that and so much more.

Sara's Family and Friends

Sara was born and raised in Cleveland, Ohio; the family—her mom, dad, and younger brother, Mark—moved to Knoxville, Tennessee, during her senior year in high school when her dad, an optician, was transferred. Her two older sisters, Liz and Maria, stayed in Ohio to attend college.

Sara's family were tremendous role models for her, a fact which she is thankful for today. From her oldest sister, Maria, Sara learned so much about life and excelling in academics. Sara says she got her "umph" from Maria's example. Thanks, Maria. She and her husband, Wayne, continue to be faith builders in our lives today.

Elizabeth, Sara's older sister by only eighteen months, can be credited with teaching Sara to never accept "no"

133

when the answer could just as well be "yes" with a little persistence.

Little brother, Mark, helped prepare Sara for becoming a mom. She had to take him to the tennis court, softball practice, and any other place he needed to go. She also took him to the public swimming pool where Sara was a lifeguard.

She handles all of our money now, and she attributes her thriftiness to her dad. You see, she was his bookkeeper as soon as she was old enough to add and subtract. And her mom taught her organizational skills and how to cook and clean house.

While she was growing up, her mother was a Roman Catholic and her father was a Baptist. She wanted to please both of them, so every Sunday she would attend Catholic Mass and then go to the Baptist Sunday school and worship service. One memory she has about church is that she ate a lot of candy that she bought with the money her dad gave her to put in the offering plate.

She was quite a tennis player and played in several regional tournaments all over the country. Hurting her back when she was seventeen ended her tennis career.

While she was playing tennis in a regional tournament as a twelve year old, she learned an invaluable lesson which we have tried to instill into our own children.

Sara had advanced all the way to the finals in her age bracket and was to play the number one seed for the championship. That girl was much better than Sara because she had more years experience on the tennis court. Sara knew she would have to play her very best to even compete with the girl.

So as the match was about to begin, she asked God to help her to win the match so she could take a trophy home to her parents. She really believed that God would give her the strength and ability to beat her opponent.

Sara played her heart out and gave the other player all she could bargain for in a tennis match. But at the end of the match, experience won over determination, and Sara lost the match.

"As my wife, Sara proves to me more and more everyday just how much God loves me."

She was ready to go home when some of her teammates asked her to stay with them while they received their trophies. After all the winners had received their awards, the master of ceremonies announced one last trophy. This trophy was for the player who best displayed sportsmanship during the tournament. The winner was Sara Copeland.

As she made her way to the podium to receive her award, Sara remembered what she had asked God to do before that last tennis match. She took a trophy home to her mom and dad, but not in the way she had planned or even prayed for. God always answers our prayer, but sometimes in ways we never imagine.

Another great influence on Sara's life continues to be her best friend, Valerie Hood. They have been friends since they were four years old and still keep in close contact today. She taught Sara so much about friendship that she still uses today in our marriage and in our family.

Valerie grew up in a family of seven children, yet she was so different and independent from her brothers and sisters. She and Sara were like salt and pepper, for wherever you saw Sara, you also saw Val. Sara is a light-skinned black woman, while Valerie is a dark-skinned black woman; salt and pepper was not a bad description.

Once before Sara sang during one of my speaking ministries a few years ago, she shared, "When I first heard this song while I was in college, I started to really pray earnestly that my friend, Valerie, would come to know Jesus as Lord and Savior of her life."

The song was one Debbie Boone recorded called "Can You Reach My Friend?" Boy, Sara sang with such conviction and commitment that I couldn't believe what I was hearing. A few short years later, God did reach her friend, Valerie, and she committed her life to Jesus Christ.

The True Story

When Sara enrolled at East Tennessee State University in Johnson City, she started attending Campus Crusade for Christ meetings led by Earle and Cara Chute. In September of 1981, she committed her life to Jesus Christ and began her Christian walk. Then just two months later, she met me. What a great reward for becoming a Christian—or more realistically, maybe it was a trial.

Well, Sara's sister Liz had a friend Lisa who wanted Sara to meet a friend of hers who was a Tennessee football player. At the time Sara was dating a guy, so she really didn't have any interest in meeting someone else. However, since this guy wasn't a Christian, Sara knew down deep in her heart that their relationship would never work out.

Lisa wouldn't take no for an answer, so finally Sara agreed to meet me on a blind date at First Apostolic Church in Knoxville. The church was having a praise and healing service, and we cried and cried together at all God did in that service.

The first time she saw me, she remembers telling our friend that I was huge, but very good looking. (I like telling this part of the story.) Well, I knew from the first time I saw her that she was going to be my wife, or else I would die trying to make her my wife.

"Lisa wouldn't take no for an answer, so finally Sara agreed to meet me on a blind date at First Apostolic Church in Knoxville."

After the service we went to get something to eat, and I asked if Sara had a boyfriend. She said yes, and I thought I would die. But I wasn't ready to give up yet.

She went back to ETSU, and we became what she calls pen pals, because we wrote and called each other on a very regular basis. I knew it was more than just pen pals, but I let her call it what she wanted. Because she was in her school marching band, she didn't attend any of my games at UT.

This went on for about two years until she went off to officer training camp for ROTC. She says she missed me so much that her heart actually ached inside just to be with me. Fortunately, while she was in boot camp, the public phone was right next to her bed. I called just about every day she was there. And while she was at boot camp, she realized she was in love with me and finally told me so. (Do you have any idea how frustrating it is to have the person you love tell you she loves you for the first time, over the telephone?)

This all happened during the summer of her junior year in college. Here I was beginning my senior year at UT, and she didn't even know I was a pretty good football player with the chance to play professional football.

Well, that September I asked Sara to marry me. I proposed to her with three dozen roses and a Coke. One of the roses just happened to be attached to a ring box. She loved my romanticism or said she did, anyway. We set our wedding date as July 27, 1985.

All Things Work Together for Good

But when she came home to Knoxville for Thanksgiving break, I told her I couldn't wait any longer and we should get married as soon as possible. She agreed, and we immediately started getting ready.

She had to get dresses for twelve bridesmaids, get the invitations out, and get the church reserved and decorated. Incredibly, she did it in less than two weeks. It must have been God's will for sure.

Another miracle that happened occurred when Sara was addressing the wedding invitations. She couldn't find the address for the minister who was going to marry us, and then, lo and behold, who appears on the television doing a commercial? Brother Billy McCool, our minister, was inviting people to attend church services at 5020 Pleasant Ridge Road. Coincidence? I don't think so.

Sara was a senior and still needed twelve hours course work to graduate; that's why she wanted to wait for our marriage until the summer when she graduated. Now she checked into transferring to Memphis State University where I was playing with the Memphis Showboats. She talked to three different counselors at MSU, who all told her there would be no problem. MSU was on the semester system just like ETSU, and both were Tennessee state universities. She could graduate on time and enroll in graduate school just as she had planned.

We got married in January in the same church where we had met and had our first date. We moved into our new condo in Memphis, and a few days later Sara went to the admissions office at Memphis State to begin her last twelve hours of study for graduation.

She was horrified when she was promptly informed that she would have to take an additional thirty-three hours of residency work at Memphis State in order to graduate. If she had known this she probably would have made me wait to get married until July. But as Paul wrote, ". . . in all things God works for the good of those who love him" (Romans 8:28). Sara graduated with a double major in marketing and management.

Our Marriage Commitment

I believe that Sara and I have a beautiful marriage which doesn't just happen on its own. Just like anything worth having, you have to work for it and we do.

> *"We got married in January in the same church where we had met and had our first date."*

People ask us what will keep our love for each other from dying. There's a very simple answer to that: Our love for each other is not based on our feelings or affection which can change or die. Our love is based on Jesus Christ who never changes even though our feelings and affections might.

Do we ever fight or disagree? Never! We simply sit down and discuss our problems like adults should. (However, people can sometimes hear our discussions from several blocks away.) Of course, we do have arguments and disagreements. But we strive like crazy to find a solution to any problem that may arise. We'll find a way to work it out.

We believe that the Bible is the basis for our faith and our very lives. When it tells us we are to marry for life, we know there must be a good reason why God hates divorce.

We are more committed to Jesus Christ than we are to each other. Believing this really puts our marriage into perspective. We also know that divorce doesn't solve anything; it simply transfers the same problems to another situation.

Many marriages fall apart because of negativism between the spouses. Sara and I work very hard to avoid negativism. Sure, there are times when we need to confront each other about faults and shortcomings, but the confrontation can take place in a positive way so as not to put each other on the defensive.

Sara has really committed herself to working hard to become that kind of Christian woman described in the Bible:

A wife of noble character who can find? She is worth far more than rubies. Her husband has full confidence in her and lacks nothing of value. She brings him good, not harm, all the days of her life. She selects wool and flax and works with eager hands. She is like the merchant ships, bringing her food from afar. She gets up while it is still dark; she provides food for her family and portions for her servant girls. She considers a field and buys it; out of her earnings she plants a vineyard. She sets about her work vigorously; her arms are strong for her tasks. She sees that her trading is profitable, and her lamp does not

---

"Many marriages fall apart because of negativism between the spouses. Sara and I work very hard to avoid negativism."

---

go out at night. In her hand she holds the distaff and grasps the spindle with her fingers. She opens her arms to the poor and extends her hands to the needy. When it snows, she has no fear for her household; for all of them are clothed in scarlet. She makes coverings for her bed; she is clothed in fine linen and purple. Her husband is respected at the city gate, where he takes his seat among the elders of the land. She makes linen garments and sells them, and supplies the merchants with sashes. She is clothed with strength and dignity; she can laugh at the days to come. She speaks with wisdom, and faithful instruction is on her tongue. She watches over the affairs of her household and does not eat the bread of idleness. Her children arise and call her blessed; her husband also, and he praises her: "Many women do noble things, but you surpass them all." Charm is deceptive, and beauty is fleeting; but a woman who fears the LORD is to be praised. Give her the reward she has earned, and let her works bring her praise at the city gate. (Proverbs 31:10–31)

Sara is not perfect, but she is working hard to be that Proverbs 31 woman. I thank God daily for bringing her into my life and for her commitment to Jesus Christ and the principles taught in the Scriptures.

I once heard someone say that your relationship with Jesus Christ can be no better than your relationship with your spouse. And on the flip side, you could also say that if your relationship with Jesus Christ is right, then your relationship with your spouse will also be right. When your commitment with Jesus Christ is in line, it's amazing how the rest of your life just seems to fall in place!

Today Sara is my personal secretary, accountant, cook, work-out partner, and ministry organizer. When you add all that together with her beautiful job of mothering Jeremy and Jecolia and being a great housekeeper, I am an incredibly fortunate husband.

MONEY AND HOPE PALACE

The Bible doesn't say that money is evil; it says that the love of money is the root of all kinds of evil. And I certainly have to agree.

The Bible tells us that we cannot serve two masters. We must choose between God and man. I have come to the basic realization that all that we have here on earth is on loan from Him. When He wants it back, we can either give it to Him, or He will take it. God has blessed me and my family with finances in order for us to be a blessing to others.

The first thing I have to do with what God has loaned to me is found in this verse:

> "Bring the whole tithe into the storehouse, that there may be food in my house. Test me in this," says the LORD Almighty, "and see if I will not throw open the floodgates of heaven and pour out so much blessing that you will not have room enough for it." (Malachi 3:10)

Some people may think the church robs its members by spending money the wrong way. We give money to God; how that church spends it has nothing to do with our motive for giving it. If that church is spending it wrongly, God will judge in due time.

I love what Steve Brown of Key Life Ministries once said, "Just because God doesn't balance the books everyday doesn't mean He isn't keeping a record." He is keeping a record and will bring judgment in his own time.

This is what tithing is to me—giving money to your local church. For me the amount of money I give to my local church is ten percent. I sincerely believe the amount you tithe to your church should be the amount the Holy Spirit lays on your heart.

Then I believe there are certain ministries and organizations that God leads me to support. To these I give offerings, which is money above and beyond the tithe to my church.

I heard somebody ask if you should tithe a percentage based on your net income or your gross income. Then I heard someone else ask if you want God to bless you on your gross or net income. Enough said.

The Bible tells us that we should lay up "a treasure in heaven that will not be exhausted, where no thief comes near and no moth destroys" (Luke 12:33). I know when I die, I am not going to be able to take a dime with me. You don't find too many U-Haul trailers behind hearses.

I also read a story a few years ago about a lady that died and wanted to be buried in her gold Lincoln Continental because she wanted to drive through the pearly gates in style. Well, we all know where that Lincoln Continental is today. It's right where it was buried.

My grandmother told me a story about two little boys standing on the beach talking to each other. The one little boy came from a wealthy family and was bragging about his riches.

He said, "See that boat out there on the water; that's my daddy's. See that big house up there on that hill; that's my daddy's. See that plane flying up there; my dad owns that airline. See that big office building down there; that's my daddy's. See that Mercedes over there; that's my daddy's."

The other little boy was getting tired of hearing all of this bragging and said, "See that water that boat is sitting on; that's my Father in heaven's. Before your daddy had anything; my Father in heaven had it all."

My grandmother's story pretty much puts everything into perspective for me. Everything I have now was God's first. Everything still belongs to God, and He can take it away anytime he sees fit. All of our finances must be used in order to benefit the kingdom of God.

The Bible also tells us that when we don't tithe, we are robbing God (Malachi 3:8). I truly believe there are going to be a lot of Christians held accountable for this fact: many people won't hear the gospel because those Christians withheld their tithes and offerings.

I know that beyond a shadow of a doubt that if God called me to the mission field or to stop playing football today and live in the inner city, I would be happy just being in His will. Money does not mean anything to Reggie White, personally. It is only a means to carry out what God has called me to do.

The NFL Strike

A lot of well-meaning Christian people criticized Sara and me for going on strike with the other NFL players a few

---

"Money does not mean anything to Reggie White, personally. It is only a means to carry out what God has called me to do."

---

years ago for "free agency." And I say Sara and me, because we are in this together, and she is as much a part of these decisions as I am.

You see, playing professional football is a lot different from most other jobs. If you don't like your job, you can quit and find another one anytime you are ready. In the

National Football League you can't do that. NFL football players are the only workers in America that don't have that privilege.

The average length of play for a NFL player is three and one half years. In baseball, basketball, golf, or hockey, players generally play much longer.

Football players, as well as other professional athletes, are actually only one play away from never playing again, and thus being out of a job. When you get hurt, a team can cut you and discontinue your salary, and there's nothing you can do about it.

When a non-Christian athlete asks for increased benefits, nobody criticizes him for getting all he can get. But when a Christian asks for more, Christians and other people alike say he is being greedy and should work for less than others.

My contract came up for negotiation in 1988 and what the Eagles were offering me was not acceptable compared to what other players of my caliber were making in the NFL. Many different offers were reported in the papers that simply were not true and yet many Christians believed what the press said and judged me rather than follow the mandate in 1 Corinthians about loving each other as believers (3:7). Love "always believes the best" about a Christian brother. They may hear that a player was offered twenty million dollars to play for six years. They don't realize that amount may be payable over twenty-five years and not the six years they play.

I'm really blessed with having two Christian agents, Kyle Rote, Jr., and Jimmy Sexton. They not only protect me legally in my professional affairs, but also spiritually.

The Bible says that "a workman is worthy of his hire." In other words, pay a man what he is worth. That's all that my agents ask when they negotiate a contract for me. Then pay Reggie White what he is worth to the Philadelphia Eagles. That's all any man can ask of his employer.

> **"I'm really blessed with having two Christian agents, Kyle Rote, Jr., and Jimmy Sexton. They not only protect me legally in my professional affairs, but also spiritually."**

The Bible says that "we should lay up treasures for an inheritance for our children." If I'm not very careful with what God has entrusted me, I am committing a sin. I know God has blessed me financially so He can use the resources He has blessed me with to bless others for the advancement of His kingdom.

Hope Palace

One of the areas of ministry that God has led Sara and me into is in establishing Hope Palace. When we bought the property where we built our house in Maryville, Tennessee, an existing house on a section of that land had six thousand square feet with seven bedrooms, eight baths, a swimming pool, and a tennis court.

We told the owners of the property we didn't want the house, but they refused to sell any part of the land to us without buying the house, too. So, we really had no choice but to buy the house, too. We had no idea what we were going to do with it.

Sara and I have always had a real love and compassion for girls having babies out of wedlock. Often ministries that help these girls avoid the murder of their babies through abortion must send the girls back to streets almost immediately after they have their babies to make room for other girls that need help. Long-term care is not available. Of course these ministries share how Jesus can make the difference, and many lives are changed through commitments made by these girls to the Lord.

We really felt that God was leading us to take this type of ministry one step farther than just helping these young women until they have their babies. Maybe we could provide the next stage.

God really impressed upon us that this house should be made available for these girls as long as they need help. I mean even after they have their babies, they can stay until permanent residence is located. If their parents want them to come back home, great, that's probably what they should do.

This idea was pretty much Sara's, but we received our confirmation of it through our pastor in New Jersey, Bruce Sofia, when he preached on Samson's mother.

An angel of the Lord came to Samson's mother and told her that she would conceive, and that she should follow strict guidelines in eating and drinking since this child would be a man of God who would deliver them from the Philistines.

She went to her husband Manoah and told him. Manoah did *not* say, "Hey, woman, God or no angel said that to me, and until he does, I doubt he really said anything to you. After all, I am the man of the house." He prayed to God that the angel would come again to teach them how to raise the child who would be born as promised (see Judges 13:1–24).

That's the position I put myself in. If God was impressing Sara that way, then I'd better move along with her or else we would miss a blessing from God. So we're just obeying God, and the house will be open for girls begin-

"God really impressed upon us that this house should be made available for these girls as long as they need help. I mean even after they have their babies."

ning in the fall of 1991. The house will be run by two house parents. As a matter of fact, volunteers from our church in Maryville will staff the positions needed to keep Hope Palace going.

Isn't it amazing how God leads you to buy something that you think you have no possible use for? Then later He reveals to you exactly why He told you to buy it. That's what happened to us about that house. God knows exactly what He is doing. We just have to listen and then obey, without reservation.

We really feel that this may be just a small part of the big picture God has laid on our hearts. God may be leading us to open many more Hope Palaces all over the country. If so, He will direct us.

Another area we feel the leading of the Lord is in ministry to gang members from the inner city. We're looking at some property far out into the wilderness as a refuge for these gang leaders and members where they can hear the message of the liberty found in Jesus Christ.

We want to minister to these young people there until they are ready to return to be an example of hope to their gangs. You see, I really believe many gang members really would like to experience new life in Jesus Christ, but they fear they will be killed if they leave their gangs.

This "hideout" I'm talking about will be the perfect place for them to go to without the fear of being killed or harmed in any way by their gangs.

I know that I want to be faithful to use what God has given me in His service. Whatever He wants to accomplish in the lives of others through me is my desire also.

FAMILY BY GOD'S DESIGN

The first couple of times Sara and I met while we were in college, I told her I wanted to have at least twelve children. She told me that she wished my poor wife, whoever she might be, good luck!

I love kids and really wouldn't mind having ten or twelve, but Sara has other ideas on that subject. However, I think she was a little worried early in our marriage. You see, she was pregnant on our first anniversary. On our second anniversary she was nursing, and she was pregnant again for our third. Then our fourth anniversary found her nursing, and she was beginning to think there was a definite trend taking place. So our fifth anniversary was a whole new experience, with no pregnancy or nursing taking place.

Seriously, we sincerely believe God's promise:

> Behold, children are a gift of the LORD; The fruit of the womb is a reward. Like arrows in the hand of a warrior, so are the children of one's youth. How blessed is the man whose quiver is full of them. . . .(Psalm 127:3–5, NAS)

Sara had a normal pregnancy with our first child who was born while we were in Memphis with the Showboats. A friend of ours with FCA suggested we read Scripture out loud to our unborn child. Amazingly, our baby would move almost every time Scripture was read.

I'll never forget being in the delivery room and feeling so helpless with Sara lying on that table being prepared for a C-section. I believe I felt every pull and poke on Sara's body. But when I peeked over the sheet and saw the beautiful creation that came from her womb, I began to cry with excitement as a baby boy appeared. His name would be Jeremy.

A couple of years later when Jecolia, was born, and I cried again for God had given us a beautiful daughter. You might ask where we got the name for our little girl. Well, Jecolia is an Old Testament name for the mother of King Jeroboam, who was one of the godly Jewish kings.

Even a Four-Year-Old Knows When He Has Sinned

An incident that happened with Jeremy recently really challenged me about confession of sin in my life.

I was sitting in my office with a friend and we were discussing what should be included in this book. As we were talking, I heard the faint sound of crying coming from outside my office doors. I looked through the glass, and there stood Jeremy, crying his eyes out.

I went to the door and opened it to see if he might be hurt. At four years old, Jeremy had to look a long way up to catch my face looking down to him.

I asked him why he was crying, and he mumbled something that I couldn't understand. So I picked him up and asked him again, "Why are you crying?"

Between the crying and sobbing, I learned that he had said a bad word. I looked at my friend sitting in my office and was a little bit embarrassed.

I explained to Jeremy why what he said was wrong and that it was good for him to be sorry for saying the word. In the back of my mind I was trying to decide if maybe I needed to spank him for saying it.

While I was still holding Jeremy, another friend who had been visiting us from New Jersey came in the study and explained what had really happened.

It seems that Jeremy was playing and did in fact say the four-letter word. No one had heard him say it. A few minutes after he uttered the unmentionable word, something inside him told him the word was wrong.

He went to my friend Frosty and told him what he had said and asked him if the word was a "bad one."

Frosty told him, "Yes, you're right, that's a bad word." Almost immediately, Jeremy broke into tears and came running to me to confess it.

If only I could be so diligent in confessing sin. How many times have we sinned and looked around to see if anyone caught us. Then when we think no one saw us, we give a sigh or relief, instead of immediately confessing it to God.

"How many times have we sinned and looked around to see if anyone caught us. Then when we think no one saw us, we give a sigh or relief, instead of immediately confessing it to God."

Sometimes I believe the measure of our maturity might be found in the time spent between committing a sin and actually confessing that sin. Thanks, Jeremy, for teaching me a valuable lesson.

Our Parenting Guidelines

Obviously, we are not expert parents, or experienced enough to relate to you the best way to raise your children. We have learned many principles which have helped us, however, and which seem to be working thus far. Let me share a few of these with you.

1. Tell your kids audibly that you love them and then show it by hugging them many times, daily.

2. Discipline your children. For willful disobedience, the punishment should be corporal. We adhere to the guideline: "He who spares the rod hates his son, but he who loves him is careful to discipline him" (Proverbs 13:24).

3. Do not use your hands to discipline, but for loving and hugging. Use another object for disciplining.

4. Never administer a spanking while you are angry. Cool down first, spank, and then love your child immediately.

5. Spend time with them, not just "quality" time, but even "unquality" time. Many nights before we go to bed, you might catch Jeremy, Jecolia, and me in a fierce wrestling match. We perform everything from "pile driving" to the "sleeper" right there on the carpet in their room.

6. Pray for your children daily. Pray for their future spouses and their future spouses' parents.

7. Love them so much that when they rebel against your authority, they'll come running back fast when they realize you did it out of love.

8. Pray for their salvation, that they will come to know the Lord while they are young.

9. Teach them to pray simple prayers. Even Jecolia, our two-year-old, can show gratitude to God with her simple prayers like "Thank you for Mommy, for

"Be consistent in your warnings. If you tell them you are going to put a pie in their face if they do something again and they do it again—put a pie in their face."

Daddy, for Jeremy, and for me, too!" Every night we have our family devotions and prayer together. I believe this is so important, and Sara and I look forward to it every night. Even when we have company, we always explain to our visitors what we are doing and excuse ourselves.

10. Teach them to trust you completely. There's a story told of a man who was a track switcher for trains. One day he was notified at the last second that a bridge was out and he needed to immediately switch the oncoming train to the other track. After he threw the switch, he looked and saw his son playing on the other track. He screamed to the top of his lungs for his son to move off the track. Would your child have obeyed immediately without question or would he have answered, "Why?" If your child won't jump to you, he doesn't trust you yet. You must instill that no-questions-asked kind of trust.

11. Teach them to ask forgiveness when they do wrong. When they confess it, teach them to repent, receive forgiveness, and learn from their mistakes.

12. Teach them to forgive whether they are asked to or not.

13. Be consistent in your warnings. If you tell them you are going to put a pie in their face if they do something again and they do it again—put a pie in their face. Be consistent. If you promise to do something, do it!

14. Never say, "You're going to get it when your dad gets home," or "I'm going to tell your father." Moms must exercise discipline as consistently as Dads.

15. Always be in agreement with each other about disciplining and always back each other up! If you disagree, don't do it in front of the children.

16. Teach kids to memorize Scripture at a very early age. We tried to get Jeremy to start memorizing verses when he was about three years old. He was having a rough time. One day we were traveling on an extended trip in our car and were listening to the gospel group, the Winans, on cassette. Jeremy was singing along with the tape, so we knew he could memorize phrases. So I said let's put the Scripture verse to a beat. I went first and then said it was Sara's turn. After Sara said Phillipians 4:13 to the beat, Jeremy wanted to try. It was unbelievable; he learned his first verse that day in the car. Jecolia memorized John 1:1 when she was only two years old. It's hard to understand her, but if you listen closely, you'll hear every word.

17. Take them to church every Sunday. Don't send them; take them and stay there with them.

18. Dads, don't be afraid to cry in front of your children. Be a man of steel—firm but gentle—willing to laugh and cry.

"Dedicate your children to God publicly, and tell them when they are older why and how you had them dedicated."

19. Tell your wife you love her in front of the children. Then kiss her, hug her, and compliment her in front of your children.

20. Let your children see their parents praying and studying Scripture together.

21. The man is the head of the home, according to Scripture, and his wife is his helpmeet, not his helpmate. The man is ultimately responsible to God for his family and their actions. The man must listen to his wife's counsel and realize she is usually right.

22. Always show a united front to your children.

23. Don't ever change a ruling your spouse has already made to your children without discussing it with your spouse in private and agreeing on the matter.

24. Dedicate your children to God publicly, and tell them when they are older why and how you had them dedicated.

25. Love the mother of your children; it's the best thing you can do for your children. There's a whole lot of truth in that old statement.

These are just some principles we have learned and are trying to instill in our children and each other. Why not sit down with your spouse and decide on the principles you wish to follow in bringing up your children?

Our Family Commitment

Not only are Sara and I committed to each other, we are also committed to our children. Their well-being is much more important than any bad feelings we could ever have about each other. When your relationship with the Lord is right, it's amazing how your relationship with your family will be right!

As you can tell from this book, I love my wife for so many different things she does. She wants both Jeremy and Jecolia to see her cleaning house and cooking dinner and grocery shopping, and not some maid doing these things. And this blesses our whole family. She really wants our children to see a woman and a mother seeking to do what God wants her to do.

Many husbands like to point out Paul's advice to wives:

> Wives, submit to your husbands as to the Lord. For the husband is the head of the wife as Christ is the head of the church, his body, of which he is the Savior. Now as the church submits to Christ, so also wives should submit to their husbands in everything. (Ephesians 5:22–24)

They would say, "Yeah, preach on, brother. I like that." But these same husbands also do not like to hear what follows:

> Husbands, love your wives, just as Christ loved the church and gave himself up for her to make her holy, cleansing her by the washing with water through the word, and to present her to himself as a radiant church, without stain or wrinkle or any other blemish, but holy and blameless. In this same way, husbands ought to love their wives as their own bodies. He who loves his wife loves himself. After all, no one ever hated his own body,

but he feeds and cares for it, just as Christ does the church. (Ephesians 5:25–28)

Uh oh, if you are a Christian husband, those last couple of verses really hit you between the eyes. I know they surely do me.

A wife is only able to submit to her husband in direct relation to how much love her husband shows toward her, just as Christ showed the church. Christ loves the church so much, that He always forgives her, always loves her unconditionally, sets a living example, and even died for her.

Wow! That's a lot of love. And yet as Christian husbands, we have no other alternative but to love our wives in the same way that Christ loved the church and gave Himself for her. I don't think there would be one single Christian, or for that matter a non-Christian, wife who would not be more than willing to submit to her husband, if he loved her in that way.

It only serves to reason that a wife cannot submit more to her husband than her husband can submit to God. Love God, love each other, and then your children will really understand your love for them.

PART ✦ FOUR

FINAL SCORE

MORE THAN WINNING!

You have heard me talk a lot about a personal relationship with Jesus Christ. If you would like to know more about how you can have this relationship, then these next few pages are for you.*

If you already have a growing relationship with Jesus Christ, but want to do everything you can to stimulate your growth even more, read the checklist at the end of this chapter.

Do You Have God's Plan for Your Life?

In most athletic contests a coach prepares a game plan ahead of time. God designed a plan for our lives before the world began. God is holy and perfect. He created us to love Him, glorify Him, and enjoy Him forever.

What is God's standard? The Bible, God's playbook, says that the standard for being on His team is to:

- Be holy. "You shall be holy, for I am holy" (1 Peter 1:16, NAS).

- Be perfect. "Be perfect, therefore, as your heavenly Father is perfect" (Matthew 5:48).

What is God's plan? God created us to:

- Love Him. "Jesus replied: 'Love the Lord your God with all your heart and with all your soul and with all your mind'" (Matthew 22:37).

---

* The text for this chapter comes from a gospel tract called "More Than Winning." ©1986. Fellowship of Christian Athletes. Used by permission. All rights reserved. Other athletically oriented ministry resources are available at (800) 289-0909.

- Glorify (honor) Him. "You are worthy, our Lord and God, to receive glory and honor and power, for you created all things, and by your will they were created and have their being" (Revelation 4:11).

- Enjoy Him forever. Jesus said, ". . . I have come that they may have life, and have it to the full" (John 10:10).

Man's Problem

Why is it that we cannot live up to God's standard of holiness and perfection and fulfill God's plan for our lives?

Because man is sinful and is separated from God.

What is sin? Sin means missing the mark, falling short of God's standard. It is not only doing wrong and failing to do what God wants (lying, gossip, losing our temper, lustful thoughts, etc.), but it is also an attitude of ignoring or rejecting God which is a result of our sinful nature. "Surely I have been a sinner from birth, sinful from the time my mother conceived me" (Psalm 51:5).

Who has sinned? "For all have sinned and fall short of the glory of God" (Romans 3:23).

What are the results of sin?

- Separation from God: "But your iniquities [sins] have separated you from your God . . . " (Isaiah 59:2).

- Death: "For the wages of sin is death . . . " (Romans 6:23).

- Judgment: "Just as man is destined to die once, and after that to face judgment" (Hebrews 9:27).

- God is holy, and we are sinful and separated from Him. Man continuously tries to reach God through his own efforts (being good, religious activities, philosophy, etc.), but, while these can be good things, they all fall short of

God's standard. "All our righteous acts [good works] are like filthy rags" (Isaiah 64:6).

God's Substitute

There is only one way to bridge this gap between God and man. God provided the only way to be on His team by sending His Son Jesus Christ as the holy and perfect substitute to die in our place.

Who is Jesus Christ?

- He is God. Jesus said, "I and the Father are one" (John 10:30).

- He is Man. ". . . the Word [Jesus] was God . . . The Word became flesh and dwelt among us" (John 1:1, 14 NAS).

What has Jesus done?

- He died as our substitute. "God demonstrates his own love for us in this: While we were still sinners, Christ died for us" (Romans 5:8).

- He rose from the dead. ". . . Christ died for our sins . . . he was buried . . . he was raised on the third day according to the Scriptures and . . . he appeared to Peter, and then to the Twelve. After that, he appeared to more than five hundred . . . " (1 Corinthians 15:3-6).

- He is the only way to God. "I am the way and the truth and the life. No one comes to the Father except through me" (John 14:6).

God has bridged the gap between Himself and man by sending Jesus Christ to die in our place as our substitute. Jesus defeated sin and death and rose from the grave. Yet, it isn't enough to just know these facts.

Man's Part

Knowing a lot about a sport and "talking the game" doesn't make you a member of a team. The same is true in becoming a Christian. It takes more than just knowing about Jesus Christ; it requires a total commitment by faith in Him.

Faith is not:

- Just knowing the facts. "You believe that there is one God. Good! Even the demons believe that—and shudder" (James 2:19).

- Just an emotional experience. Raising your hands or repeating a prayer is not enough.

Faith is:

- Repenting. Turning to God from sin: "Godly sorrow brings repentance that leads to salvation and leaves no regret . . . " (2 Corinthians 7:10).

- Receiving Jesus Christ. Trusting in Christ alone for salvation. "Yet to all who received him, to those who believed in his name, he gave the right to become children of God" (John 1:12).

On which side do you see yourself? Where would you like to be?

Jesus said, "I tell you the truth, whoever hears my word and believes him who sent me has eternal life and will not be condemned; he has crossed over from death to life." (John 5:24).

Replay of God's Plan

What is this commitment of faith in Jesus Christ all about?

- Realize God is holy and perfect; we are sinners and cannot save ourselves.

- Recognize who Jesus is and what He's done as our sub-stitute.

- Repent by turning to God from sin.

- Receive Jesus Christ by faith as Savior and Lord. "Yet to all who received him, to those who believed in his name, he gave the right to become children of God" (John 1:12).

- Respond to Jesus Christ in a life of obedience. "If anyone would come after me, he must deny himself and take up his cross daily and follow me" (Luke 9:23).

Does God's plan make sense to you? Are you willing to repent and receive Jesus Christ? If so, express to God your need for Him. If you're not sure what to say, consider the suggested prayer of commitment which follows. Remember that God is more concerned with your attitude than with the words you say.

- *Suggested Prayer of Commitment*:

  Lord Jesus, I need You. I realize I'm a sinner and I can't save myself. I need Your mercy. I believe that You died on the cross for my sins and rose from the dead. I re-pent of my sins and put my faith in You as Savior and Lord. Take control of my life and help me to follow You in obedience. In Jesus' name, Amen.

"If you confess with your mouth, 'Jesus is Lord,' and believe in your heart that God raised him from the dead, you will be saved . . ." for "everyone who calls on the name of the Lord will be saved" (Romans 10:9, 13).

Know Your Position

Once you have committed your life to Jesus Christ, it is im-portant to understand what your position is on His team. Too many people make the mistake of measuring the certainty of their salvation by their feelings instead of the facts of God's Word.

In Jesus Christ you have a new life. See what God's Word says about your new position on His team:

N—I am a *New Creation* in Christ (2 Corinthians 5:17; Galatians 2:20).

E—I have *Everything* I need for life and godliness (2 Peter 1:3, Ephesians 1:3).

W—I am a *Witness* for Christ and am His *Workmanship*, created for good works (Acts 1:8; Ephesians 2:10).

L—I am *Loved* and accepted completely in Christ (Ephesians 1:6; Romans 8:39).

I—I am *Indwelt* by the Holy Spirit (1 Corinthians 6:19–20; 1 John 4:4).

F—I am *Forgiven* and *Free* from condemnation (1 John 1:9; Romans 8:1–2).

E—I have *Eternal* Life in Christ (John 5:24; 1 John 5:11, 13).

Trust God! Put your faith in His Word, not in your feelings. "I write these things to you who believe in the name of the Son of God so that you may know that you have eternal life" (1 John 5:13).

Seven Daily Exercises

Just as physical growth demands physical exercise, spiritual growth as a Christian demands spiritual exercise. To build spiritual muscle here are seven daily exercises:

1. *Daily Die to Self.* ". . . In Christ Jesus our Lord, I die daily"(1 Corinthians 15:31, NAS).

2. *Daily Obedience to Christ.* "Then he said to them all: 'If anyone would come after me, he must deny himself and

take up his cross daily and follow me'"(Luke 9:23). Every day commit yourself to obeying God and His Word.

3. Daily Bible Reading. "They . . . examined the Scriptures every day"(Acts 17:11). Spend time every day reading God's Word. First read through the Gospel of John, one chapter per day.

4. Daily Prayer. ". . . give us this day our daily bread"(Matthew 6:11, NAS). Devote time every day talking to God in prayer.

5. Daily Fellowship. "Encourage one another daily"(Hebrews 3:13). Get involved with your local church and seek regular fellowship with other Christians.

6. Daily Witnessing. "Day after day . . . they never stopped teaching and proclaiming the good news that Jesus is the Christ"(Acts 5:42). Witness for Christ every day through your words and actions.

7. Daily Praise. "Seven times a day I praise you"(Psalm 119:164). Every day praise God for who He is and what He has done.

Do these exercises and you will grow strong in your Christian life and be an effective member of God's team.

If you prayed the prayer mentioned above or you would like more information about this relationship with Jesus Christ, tell me about it. Write to me at this address:

Reggie White
Alpha and Omega Ministries
P. O. Box 4336
Maryville, Tennessee 37802.

Alan Herd, a friend of mine with the Fellowship of Christian Athletes, came up with this list of poignant statements that just might prick your conscience in an area that will bring you closer in your walk with the Lord. If you see yourself in any of these situations, you need to take the steps necessary to get right with God.

- When things must be done your way and only your way.
- When you lead by force rather than by love.
- When everything done around you must have your stamp of approval.
- When you can't trust others who are capable without constantly checking on them.
- When you manipulate to get your own way.
- When you believe that you are the only one that can get the job done.
- When you believe that God can only work through you.
- When you believe that God must check with you first to see if His plan is OK.
- When in your own strength you try knocking down a door that God has closed.
- When all else fails, you push through anyway.
- When you must accomplish God's will no matter who gets hurt in the process.
- When you believe you are the only one God truly loves.
- When your time alone with the Lord is measured in minutes and hours rather than what He says to you.
- When it's hard to admit you are wrong.
- When you admit you are wrong, and then must turn it into a sermon so that others can see how godly you are.
- When it is a chore to be selfless.
- When you keep a running score of how you have helped others.

- When your time frame and God's are different, and you don't care.

- When you think your mansion in heaven will be greater than others.

- When you believe years of service equal years of growth.

- When you hope that God's blessings are mostly material.

- When you are more concerned with the outward appearance than the heart of the matter.

- When God's Word becomes a tool for your use.

- When you believe God's plan will fail without your help.

- When you help others and think how fortunate they are to have you as a friend.

- When pleasing others equals pleasing God.

- When material gain is as important as winning souls for Christ.

- When admitting you are wrong is the same as admitting defeat.

- When you must go out of your way to convince your family that you love them.

- When you pray aloud to God and hope that others enjoyed your prayers.

- When you believe that you have earned the right to indulge yourself.

- When sin is not as serious as it used to be.

- When your comfort level is non-negotiable.

- When you believe the cross you bear is a way to promote yourself.

- When you make a habit of following the path of least resistance.

- When a waitress isn't a person but someone destined to serve you.

- When you know that you are selfish, and it becomes an excuse rather than a sin.

- When you believe that others must pay their dues just as you did.

- When you inwardly smile when someone fails doing something you didn't agree with.

- When you expect more from others than you do from yourself.

- When you are in charge of an event, and your reputation is on the line instead of God's.

- When you blow up inwardly over little annoyances.

- When you believe one mistake can spoil God's plan.

- When you appreciate others for what they can do for you rather than who they are.

- When you scratch someone's back just to get yours scratched in return.

- When you count others' mistakes more than their successes.

- When an A- is good enough for you but not for others.

- When you feel as if it's your personal job to improve someone else.

- When you are disappointed even though Jesus is not.

- When two ice cubes in your tea aren't enough and you let everyone else know about it.

- When you pride yourself on being practical.

- When you pride yourself as a people person, but others don't.

- When "He that began a good work in you" isn't working it fast enough in others.

- When you are complimented and forget Whom to praise.

- When you take pride in your humility.

Take the time right now to talk with Jesus about these areas of your life as the Holy Spirit leads you. Remember:

> Therefore, since we are surrounded by such a great cloud of witnesses, let us throw off everything that hinders and the sin that so easily entangles, and let us run with perseverance the race marked out for us. (Hebrews 12:1)

My pastor in New Jersey, Bruce Sofia, explained to me why growing Christians are so harshly criticized. He said it's because the persons doing the criticizing really do want to see those Christians be all they are supposed to be.

He's right! So just live out your convictions. When you fail, and you are certainly going to, confess, repent, and move on!

May God richly bless you as you obey Him!

REGGIE WHITE
Acts 4:12; 2 Corinthians 7:9-11

PROFESSIONAL FOOTBALL CAREER STATISTICS

(Excerpted from the *Philadelphia Eagles Media Guide* 1989 & 1990 and used by permission.)

REGGIE WHITE, DE
Tennessee; 6-5; 285; Born: 12/19/61
Supp. Draft 1, 1984; Year Eagle: 7; Year NFL: 7

1990 Season

One of the most dominant defensive players in the game today, Reggie White was selected for the fifth consecutive season as a starter in the Pro Bowl, earned near unanimous All-NFL acclaim, was also selected as the defensive lineman of the year by the NFL Players' Association. . . . For the fifth consecutive year was named to the All-Madden Team . . . His fourteen sacks paced the Birds, were second in the NFC to 49ers' Charles Haley, and fourth in the NFL . . . had at least a partial sack in ten games including a season high three sack performance vs. Ind . . . registered his first career interception off a deflected pass vs. Wash. in a MNF matchup and returned it thirty-three yards . . . at LA Rams, sacked Jim Everett forcing a fumble which Jerome Brown recovered and led to the game's first points. Four time Mackey Award winner for best defensive lineman.

Pro Career: In just six NFL seasons, Reggie has established himself as one of the top linemen ever to play in the NFL . . . since entering the NFL in 1985, his 95.0 sacks lead all NFL players (1.1 per game) . . . "He's the best defensive lineman I've ever been around," said Buddy Ryan—high praise from one who has coached the likes of John Elliott (Jets), Alan Page and Carl Eller (Vikings), Dan Hampton and Richard Dent (Bears) . . . the only player to be selected by *Pro Football Weekly* to the 1980's All-Decade Team and projected to be on the 1990s All-Decade Team . . . with his excellent strength and speed for a 285-pounder (4.6 in the 40), White can wreak havoc on offensive blocking schemes by lining up anywhere along the line as he does in the various Eagles' defenses, although he most often plays LDE . . .

1989 Season

Reggie was selected to start in the AFC-NFC Pro Bowl and also was named first team All-NFL (AP, *College and Pro Football Newsweekly, Football Digest, Pro Football Weekly*, and *Sports Illustrated)* and first team All-NFC *(Football News, Pro Football Weekly* and UPI) . . . had three multiple sack games, including season-high 2.5 against 49ers (9-24) . . . recorded eleven sacks and eighty-two hurries to help defense set team record with sixty-two sacks . . . registered 123 tackles for second straight 100+ tackle season despite double- and triple-teaming . . . forced a fumble by Giants' QB Phil Simms that was picked up and returned for a TD on opening series of matchup between NFC East leaders at NY (12/3) . . .

1988 Season

Reggie led the NFL in sacks for second straight year . . . named NFL Player of the Year by the Washington Touchdown Club and was selected unaminously by his peers to start in the AFC-NFC Pro Bowl . . . finished second to Chicago's Mike Singletary in the AP balloting for the NFL's most valuable defensive player and gained near unanimous first team All-NFL recognition . . . had six multiple sack games, including the third four-sack game of his career (at Minn. 9/25) . . . collected 10.5 sacks in the final eight games . . . his 133 tackles led all Eagles' linemen . . . his fourteen stops along with two QB sacks at Dallas in the season finale earned him NFC defensive player of the week honors en route to also receiving NFC defensive-player-of-the-month recognition (Dec.) . . . Third time Mackey Award winner.

1987 Season

Reggie led the League with an NFC-record twenty-one sacks and fell just one short of the NFL single-season mark (twenty-two by Jets' Mark Gastineau in 1984) . . . was also named the NFL defensive player of the year by NFL Films, The Newspaper Enterprise Association, and *Touchdown* . . . in addition, earned NFC defensive player of the year honors from UPI, *Pro Football Weekly,* and the Kansas City 101 Club, and defensive linemen of the year recognition from the NFL alumni . . . also earned first team All-NFL honors from AP, *The Sporting News,* the Pro Football Writers Association, *Pro Football Weekly,* NFL Films, and the NEA . . . was selected by his peers as a starter for the Pro Bowl . . . also was voted the Eagles' defensive MVP by his teammates . . . recorded a sack in all but one of the twelve games in which he played and registered nine multiple sack games . . . in the season opener at Wash., stole the ball from QB Doug Williams and ran seventy yards for a TD (his first as an Eagle) . . . Second time Mackey Award winner.

1986 Season

Reggie capped an outstanding season by being selected starting defensive end in the Pro Bowl and was then named

MVP of that game when he tied a Pro Bowl record with four sacks . . . also earned first team All-NFL and first team All-NFC honors . . . ranked third in both the NFL and NFC in sacks (eighteen, then an Eagles' record) behind Lawrence Taylor (20.5) and Dexter Manley (18.5) . . . made fifteen of his eighteen sacks over the latter half of the season . . . registered three sacks at Dallas en route to NFC defensive player of the week honors . . .

1985 Season

Reggie officially became an Eagle on 9/20 when Birds purchased rights from Memphis Showboats of the USFL . . . joined club in week four and went on to be named NFC defensive rookie of the year by players, first team NFL all-rookie, and honorable mention All-Pro. NFL debut vs. NYG on 9/29 included 2.5 sacks and deflected pass that was intercepted by Herman Edwards and returned for TD . . . became starting LDE in Birds' then 3-4 defense the following week . . . finished season tied for Eagles' lead with thirteen sacks (fifth in NFC) prior to joining Birds, played in twenty regular and postseason games for Showboats . . . named first team All-USFL after ranking third in league with 12.5 sacks . . . Mackey Rookie of the Year.

1984 Season

Began pro career with Memphis in January and made USFL all-rookie team after recording eleven sacks . . . Eagles selected him as their first choice (fourth overall) in the NFL's supplemental draft.

Career Statistics

Year	Club	Gp/Gs	Tackles			Quarterback	
			Solo	Asst	Tot	Sacks	Hurries
1984	Memphis	16/16	52	43	95	11.0	N/A
1985	Memphis	18/18	68	30	98	12.5	N/A
USFL Totals		34/34	120	73	193	23.5	N/A
1985	Phil.	13/12	62	38	100	13.0	N/A
1986	Phil.	16/16	83	15	98	18.0	52
1987	Phil.	12/12	62	14	76	21.0	48
1988	Phil.	16/16	96	37	133	18.0	70
1989	Phil.	16/16	82	41	123	11.0	82
1990	Phil.	16/16	59	24	83	14.0	62
NFL Totals		89/88	444	169	613	95.0	314

Additional Stats

- Touchdowns (1 USFL, 1 NFL)—vs. Birm. 5/3/85 (Returned fumble 30 yards), at Wash; (NFL) 9/13/87 (recorded a sack of QB Doug Williams, a forced fumble, and a seventy-yard return of a fumble for a TD all on one play)

- Safeties (1)—vs. Wash. 12/8/85 (forced QB Jay Schroeder into intentional grounding from end zone)

- Blocked field goals (2)—vs. NYG 10/12/86; vs. St.L. 12/7/86

- Blocked PAT (1)—vs. Atl. 10/30/88.

- Career Highs: Tackles—Total 14 (twice) last at Dal. 12/16/88; Solo—11 at Dal. 12/16/88; Sacks—4 (three times) last at Min. 9/25/88.

The typeface for the text of this book is *Palatino*. This type—best known as a contemporary *italic* typeface—was a post-World War II design crafted by the talented young German calligrapher Hermann Zapf. For inspiration, Zapf drew upon the writing legacy of a group of Italian Renaissance writing masters, in which the typeface's namesake, Giovanni Battista Palatino, was numbered. Giovanni Palatino's *Libro nuovo d'imparare a scrivera* was published in Rome in 1540 and became one of the most used, wide-ranging writing manuals of the sixteenth century. Zapf was an apt student of the European masters, and contemporary *Palatino* is one of his contributions to modern typography.

Substantive Editing:
Cynthia Tripp

Copy Editing:
Cynthia Tripp

Cover Design:
Steve Diggs & Friends
Nashville, Tennessee

Page Composition:
Xerox Ventura Publisher
Linotronic L-100 Postscript® Imagesetter

Printing and Binding:
Maple-Vail Book Manufacturing Group,
York, Pennsylvania

Cover Printing:
Strine Printing Company
York, Pennsylvania